Effective
Postgraduate
Supervision

Effective Postgraduate Supervision

Improving the
Student–Supervisor Relationship

Adrian R. Eley and
Roy Jennings

Open University Press

Open University Press
McGraw-Hill Education
McGraw-Hill House
Shoppenhangers Road
Maidenhead
Berkshire
England
SL6 2QL

e-mail: enquiries@openup.co.uk
world wide web: www.openup.co.uk

and Two Penn Plaza, New York, NY 10121-2289, USA

First published 2005

A catalogue record of this book is available from the British Library

ISBN-13: 978 0335 217076 (pb)   978 0335 217083 (hb)
ISBN-10: 0335 21707 9 (pb)   0335 21708 7 (hb)

Library of Congress Cataloging-in-Publication Data
CIP data has been applied for

Typeset by RefineCatch Limited, Bungay, Suffolk
Printed in Poland EU by OZGraf. S.A. www.polskabook.pl

To Jean and Derek Eley (Adrian Eley)

To all my postgraduate research students
past and present (Roy Jennings)

Contents

Foreword   ix
Preface   xi
Acknowledgements   xiii
Contributors   xv

Introduction   1

 1 An Issue of Isolation   7
    Penny Simons
 2 An Issue of Conflict   12
 3 An Issue of Non-Compliance   17
 4 An Issue of Plagiarism   21
 5 An Issue of Time   27
 6 An Issue of Language   32
 7 An Issue of Writing   37
    Mick Hattaway
 8 An Issue of Scrutiny   43
 9 An Issue of Transfer   48
10 An Issue of Progress   53
11 An Issue of Judgement   57
12 An Issue of Distance   62
    Jerry Wellington
13 An Issue of Teaching   69
14 An Issue of Management   73
15 An Issue of Culture   77
16 An Issue of Funding   82
17 An Issue of Appeal   88
18 An Issue of Stability   92
19 An Issue of Ownership   97
20 An Issue of Availability   101
21 An Issue of Health   106

22	An Issue of Direction	110
23	An Issue of Contract	115
24	An Issue of Priority	120
25	An Issue of Write-Up	124
26	An Issue of *Viva* Preparation	129
27	An Issue of Identity	136
	Jackie Marsh	
28	An Issue of Alleged Fraud	142
29	An Issue of Collaboration	148
30	An Issue of Procedure	156
31	Conclusions	162

Key Questions	168
Appendix 1: Answers to the Key Questions	171
Appendix 2: Use of Student–Supervisor Issues in a Workshop Setting	179
Bibliography	185
Index	187

Foreword

Postgraduate research degrees and the challenges of effective supervision are high on the agenda of many higher education institutions. It is now normal for institutions to require new supervisors to be trained before supervising students; some institutions now require regular continuing professional development for existing supervisors. However, this training barely scratches the surface of the potential challenges facing supervisors, particularly given the diversity of researches, research degree provision and the more demanding 'customer culture' today. The days of acquiring knowledge by sitting at the feet of a great researcher are long gone.

This book is written as a handy reference of case studies of potential issues encountered in research degree supervision. Some are more extreme than others, and hopefully no one supervisor will encounter them all. However, they do provide a useful framework to think about the complexities of being an effective supervisor, irrespective of your previous experience.

If you are an experienced supervisor, you will recognize some case histories as similar to your own or colleagues' experiences. There may be others you have yet to come across. Use this book as a handy reference source to consider how to engage with your researchers and to give advice to others.

If you are a new supervisor, I urge you not to read this book cover-to-cover: the cumulative effect of these issues all at once would be too depressing! You will be unlikely, or very unlucky, to encounter many of the situations in this book. But prevention is always better than cure, so do dip into it as you find yourself in new situations. You can use the case histories as a way to avoid any potential issues by being aware of the pitfalls and setting up structures and procedures to prevent them in advance.

This book is also of relevance to trainers, staff developers and others responsible for providing support for supervisors. The book describes how case histories can easily be adapted to become discussion topics for workshops. Those responsible for quality assuring research degree programmes could also use the book to reflect on whether their procedures are robust enough to minimize the risk of these issues happening in their institutions.

Finally, the supervisory process is not a one-sided relationship. For it to work well, there must be responsibilities on both sides. Many of the case histories are equally useful to illustrate to doctoral researchers the challenges of building a successful relationship and their part in ensuring that this happens.

This book is an excellent way of sharing some of the depth and wealth of experience we have in providing research supervision within the UK.

Janet Metcalfe
Director, UK GRAD Programme

Preface

Having worked since 1972 as, first, a Lecturer, then successively as a Senior Lecturer, Reader and finally Professor, in the University of Sheffield Medical School, by the mid-1990s Roy Jennings had supervised, in all but one instance successfully, 27 home-based or overseas students for PhD or Master's degrees. Roy enjoyed, and indeed continues to gain much pleasure, from the very varied experiences of supervision. These include setting up effective, working relationships with graduate students of widely differing personalities from many different backgrounds and cultures, through the thrills and disappointments of the research experience, the feeling of assisting in the research training and development of enthusiastic and highly motivated individuals, to the emergence of these young persons to take up a career, not always as a researcher, but certainly in situations that could be of benefit both to them and, in some small way, to the global community as a whole. Roy would like to think that all his graduate students have enjoyed their experiences of research training, at least when looking back, if not at the time!

In the 1990s, Roy became a member, and then Chair for four years, of the University of Sheffield Faculty of Medicine Higher Degrees Committee, and was in a position to appreciate the many types of interaction and problematic situations that can arise at any stage in a student–supervisor research programme.

Roy's expertise, experience and knowledge of research supervision were brought home to him in 1996 when it was suggested he might like to become involved in the delivery of a series of workshops primarily to newly-appointed academic staff with little experience of research supervision. With the excellent help and advice of Joyce Godfrey at the Staff Development Unit at the University of Sheffield, these workshops, and their several formats, were duly devised and delivered to many departments in several Faculties of the university over a number of years.

The workshops proved highly successful and useful, and were attended not just by the younger members of academic staff, but also by more senior academics, usually with considerable experience in research supervision, together with a sprinkling of graduate students. This mix at most of the workshops of younger and more mature heads always seemed to promote valuable and enjoyable discussions, and often revelations from the more experienced participants of new and illuminating angles on a number of the problems of research supervision. Everyone involved, including Roy, seemed to gain increased understanding of the nature of the research supervision process, the vagaries, the unforeseen difficulties and surprises that can arise in the three or so years of a student–supervisor working relationship, and the means by which at least some of the awkward situations that may arise can be resolved.

Since becoming Lecturer in 1987 and then Senior Lecturer, Adrian has also successfully supervised 27 home-based or overseas students for PhD or Master's degrees. In 2001, Adrian was awarded the university's MEd in Teaching and Learning which included a thesis on 'The Student/Supervisor Relationship'. Since then he has become Chair of the Graduate Research Committee of the School of Medicine and more recently Sub-Dean for Post-graduate Affairs (and Chair of the Graduate Research Committee) of the Faculty of Medicine.

Following Roy's highly successful workshops on research supervision, Adrian suggested that Issues similar to those used in the workshops might form the basis of a case study-based book. After several discussions, plans for a book were outlined and eventually *Effective Postgraduate Supervision: Improving the Student–Supervisor Relationship* was born. This book is the product of these successful workshops and the many years of experience of both authors in improving the student–supervisor relationship for both parties to the interaction. We hope you will find it of interest.

Roy Jennings and Adrian Eley
University of Sheffield
February 2005

Acknowledgements

In the preparation of this book, we would like to thank several people. First, we are grateful to our four contributors (Professor Mick Hattaway, Dr Jackie Marsh, Dr Penny Simons and Professor Jerry Wellington) who each provided an Issue and the benefits of their experience in helpful discussions. Professor Jennings would particularly like to acknowledge the skill and expertise of Joyce Godfrey from the Staff Development Unit, who was instrumental in developing earlier case studies for use in supervisor workshops. We are grateful for the support and advice of Peter Fearnley from the Graduate Research Office who gave important feedback on a draft of the complete text. Dr Eley would particularly like to thank his wife, Dr Penny Eley, from the Department of French, for valuable discussions and development of certain Issues.

We are especially indebted to a number of colleagues from institutions in the UK for providing information on guidelines for postgraduate research degrees. This book would not have been possible without the support and guidance of Shona Mullen and Melanie Smith from Open University Press. Finally, the authors would like to thank Gillian Griffiths for her word-processing skills which have resulted in the production of the final version of this text.

Disclaimer

Contributors

Adrian Eley, MSc, MEd, Phd is Senior Lecturer in Medical Microbiology and Sub-Dean for Postgraduate Affairs in the Faculty of Medicine at the University of Sheffield. He is interested in all aspects of postgraduate research activities, particularly those related to supervision and has successfully supervised postgraduate research students since 1987.

Mick Hattaway, MA, PhD, FEA, is Professor of English Literature at the University of Sheffield. He has many years experience of supervising several postgraduate students.

Roy Jennings, BSc, PhD is Emeritus Professor at the University of Sheffield where he was Professor of Virology from 1996 to 2000. He was a member, and then chair, of the Graduate Research Committee in the Faculty of Medicine for nine years and has supervised postgraduate research students since 1967.

Jackie Marsh, BA, PGCE, MEd, PhD, is Senior Lecturer in Education at the University of Sheffield. She has experience of supervising several postgraduate students and contributes to the School of Education's EdD Programme.

Penny Simons, MA, PhD, is Senior Lecturer in French at the University of Sheffield. She has experience of supervising postgraduate students as well as devising and implementing training programmes for research supervisors in the Arts and Humanities.

Jerry Wellington, BA, MA, PhD, is Professor of Education at the University of Sheffield. He is currently Head of Research Degrees in the School of Education and teaches methodology, research methods and academic writing to MEd, MPhil/PhD and EdD students. He has many years experience of supervising postgraduate students.

Introduction

Higher research degrees in the UK

The past few years have seen an increase in the number of postgraduate research students in the UK, in particular those coming from overseas. At the same time, doctoral degree provision is no longer restricted to the PhD, with the emergence of the 'New Route' PhD or PhD with Integrated Studies, and the growth of professional doctorates. As a result, more academic staff, often to a greater extent than before, have supervisory responsibilities. Moreover, the emergence of new disciplines and the increased volume and quality of research in the 'new' universities have resulted in many opportunities for postgraduate research and the emergence of inexperienced supervisors. At the same time there are internal growth targets for numbers of postgraduate research students and external pressures from funding bodies for successful and rapid completion of research degrees and for early publication of research work in the quality journals.

In turn, these funding bodies have put additional pressures on research students. Furthermore, in response to government and Research Councils' concerns about the employment prospects of research students, doctoral students are now expected to acquire a wide range of employment-related or so-called transferable skills.

Not surprisingly, these increasing demands on both supervisors and students are likely to put an extra strain on the student–supervisor relationship. Before we consider the nature of this relationship, it is important to reflect on the role of the supervisor.

Role of the supervisor

A supervisor can have many roles, including those of director, adviser, teacher, guide, tutor, critic etc. Not only can these roles change during the doctoral programme but they may be influenced by disciplinary cultures. In simple terms, differences are apparent, for example, between the Arts and the Sciences. The supervision style adopted in the Arts and Sciences – hands off as opposed to hands on – mimics the communication style of the disciplines where academics in the Arts tend to be more individualistic and less likely to work in teams than their Science colleagues. Similarly, the different frequencies and regularities of supervisory meetings between academics and students in the Arts and the Sciences match the mode of communication between academics in those disciplines. The publication rates of students and the extent to which students publish jointly with their supervisors also differ between the Arts and the Sciences and these differences again mimic the practice of academics in these subject areas.

Many academics consider it important for supervision to be seen as a teaching as well as a research role. Within this teaching role, giving criticism is one of the main activities that a supervisor has to undertake. Apart from being specific about what precisely is wrong with a student's performance, it is also necessary to know what kind of criticism is appropriate at a given point in a student's research career. The reason for giving criticism effectively is that, through it, students can eventually learn how to evaluate their own work and thus undergo self-development. Also, helping students become academically independent by introducing such a process of weaning is fundamental to the supervisory process.

It is particularly important to supervisors to know what students expect of them. According to Phillips and Pugh (2000), students expect supervisors to do the following:

- to read work well in advance;
- to be available when needed;
- to be friendly, open and supportive;
- to be constructively critical;
- to have a good knowledge of the research area;
- to structure meetings so that it is relatively easy to exchange ideas;
- to have sufficient interest in their research to guide the student towards more information;
- to act as a role model;
- to help their academic role development.

If supervisors are aware of the above, and students understand what supervisors expect of them, then there will be a basis for the development of a successful student–supervisor relationship.

The student–supervisor relationship

This relationship has always been fundamental to research degree study, yet received little attention in the literature until recently. However, growing scrutiny of this area has meant that the supervisory relationship has developed a higher research profile. A review of supervisory practices by Dryden and Jones (1991) has indicated a number of criticisms such as:

- *Lack of attention to process issues.* It has been argued that supervisors have tended to neglect issues related to the process of research degree study. There has been a need for attention to writing skills, and the need to demystify all aspects of research degree study, and to facilitate students' acquisition of skills, such as the ability to manage time and seek realistic goals and the ability to communicate both verbally and in writing. It has also been pointed out that it is unlikely that supervisors will easily be able to facilitate such developments in their students unless supervisors themselves receive some form of training in these areas.
- *Confusion over roles.* Another major area relating to problems with supervision involves lack of clarity between staff and students concerning their respective roles. For example, both student and supervisor can harbour differing perceptions of what each should be doing and problems can ensue as a consequence. To clarify this, there has been emphasis on the importance of agreeing at the outset of a study an explicit formal contract that identifies respective rights and obligations.
- *Interpersonal problems.* Isolation has been identified on a number of occasions as a major problem for research students, especially in certain subject areas. Additional problems may also be faced by students who do not conform to the traditional white middle-class, heterosexual, male student model. With the increasing rise in numbers of overseas students recruited, it is important to explore some of the implications for doctoral provision in the light of an increasingly heterogeneous student population.
- *Problems with the traditional supervisory model.* Finally, criticisms have been made of the narrowness of the traditional one-to-one supervision relationship, although increasingly supervisory teams are more commonly seen. To help remedy this, there has been emphasis on the educational importance of providing opportunities for students to participate in workshop-based activities with other students and the intellectual and social importance of developing collegiality within doctoral study. Perhaps the student–supervisor relationship should be necessarily asymmetrical and the ultimate aim should be to see the power imbalance reduce and level out as the student moves gradually from the position of apprentice to one of colleague.

It has been suggested that most supervisors seem to find for themselves an optimum level of involvement and interaction, although this may not be ideal for the student. Moreover, this optimum level may take years of experience to achieve and could be problematic to students during this supervisor learning period.

If students are to do well, they must understand what their supervisors expect of them. According to Delamont et al. (2004) and Phillips and Pugh (2000), the following set of expectations are probably fairly general among supervisors. Supervisors expect:

- their students to be independent;
- their students to produce good quality written work;
- to have regular meetings with their research students;
- their research students to be honest when reporting on their progress;
- their research students to follow the advice that they give, when it has been at the request of the student;
- their students to be enthusiastic about their work.

New developments in UK graduate education

In the UK there have been many developments since the *Guidelines on the Quality Assurance of Research Degrees* was published by HEQC in 1996. Perhaps the most important was the Quality Assurance Agency (QAA) for Higher Education's *Code of Practice for the Assurance of Academic Quality and Standards in Higher Education* (1999). One of the sections was on Postgraduate Research Programmes and this was published in 1999 in response to the Report of the National Committee of Inquiry into Higher Education (the Dearing Report) (1997). The Code assumes that by taking into account principles and practices agreed nationally, institutions will have their own systems for independent verification of both quality and standards and of the effectiveness of quality assurance systems.

Recently there have been several publications including the *SET for Success* report (April 2002), improving standards in postgraduate research degree programmes (HEFCE 03/23), and skills training requirements for research students (published as Annex A to HEFCE 03/23). In response to these publications, a revised section on Postgraduate Research Programmes of the Code was published in September 2004 (QAA 2004). Of particular note was a circular letter published by the Higher Education Funding Council for England (HEFCE) in September 2004, in which it was stated that the establishment of minimum standards for postgraduate research degree programmes will be linked to funding.

Often institutions have had their own expectations of standards which need to be achieved in postgraduate research programmes. In the past and without national guidelines, there was considerable variation among institutions in this area. However, with the development of a national Code of Practice which will be linked to funding, greater parity between institutional provision is now inevitable.

A new development in the way student complaints that cannot be resolved at the institutional level are now being handled in England and Wales has been the creation of the Office of the Independent Adjudicator for Higher Education. From January 2005 all complaints have been handled by this body as the Visitor scheme no longer takes on new cases. All higher education institutions in England and Wales are required to comply with the Rules of the scheme.

Another institutional response to concerns about the quality of postgraduate education, especially about research students' submission times, has been the emergence of graduate schools or their equivalents, which are now found in the majority of institutions. In a report by the UK Council for Graduate Education in 1995, a graduate school was defined as 'a distinct organization concerned with the promotion of high quality graduate education and the administration of graduate education within an institution or across a number of institutions'. Institutions have found them to be a convenient way to manage postgraduate provision and to provide a focus for change in provision, often in response to national initiatives.

Although the emphasis of doctoral provision is still the PhD, there has been a growing trend to introduce professional doctorates. These offer more taught provision with less emphasis on research. In general, these degrees appeal to more mature students who gain them principally to seek advancement in their career rather than focusing on gaining research expertise.

Another variation in doctoral provision has been the recent introduction of the 'New Route' PhD or PhD with Integrated Studies which is usually a four-year programme which includes taught Master's training as well as a PhD. Obviously there are similarities here with more traditional one- and three-year Master's and PhD programmes, although the integrated nature of the 'New Route' PhD allows for more of a focus on research training throughout the programme. Supervisors now need to be aware of the demands and expectations of the different doctoral programmes.

Finally, an issue with considerable repercussions on doctoral programmes is that of research governance and good practice. Essentially this means that research projects must meet the necessary standards for university research as specified in respective policies and procedures. Moreover, ethics approval is now required for projects involving all human participants even if the NHS is not involved. It is important to remember that it is the responsibility of the supervisor to ensure that the necessary ethical approval has been obtained before research students can undertake their projects.

Aims of the text

This text is not intended to be a comprehensive book on research supervision, but has been written in the style of a practical guide to help supervisors deal with supervisory problem situations. It is aimed primarily at university academic staff who have a responsibility for postgraduate research supervision. Essentially, the book is a series of case studies which typically reflects common problems encountered in the student–supervisor relationship. The case studies follow this brief introduction to the book. Scenarios provide the background to the case studies. These scenarios are then analysed, with advice given on how problems may be prevented or resolved. Discussion of the main themes of the case studies is given in the Evolution of the Problem section, followed by a list of strategies for possible prevention and resolution of the problem. A Key Question from each Issue is provided at the back of the book, and in Appendix 1, considered responses to the Key Question are outlined.

In Appendix 2 there is a comprehensive description, with examples, of how case studies can be used in a workshop environment to promote supervisor development.

The authors realize that there will be differences in institutional practice and although we have consulted widely in the UK, it is possible that some case studies might be handled differently elsewhere. Naturally, we respect other views and opinions. What we portray is representative of our experience.

Of course this book is not written exclusively for research supervisors and the nature of the student–supervisor relationship means that research students will also find it of relevance to them.

1

An Issue of Isolation

Penny Simons

Scenario

Becky had really enjoyed her undergraduate studies at the University of the Midlands and graduated with a good first-class degree. She had a lively group of friends and found her course in medieval history completely fascinating. When her favourite teacher, the eminent medieval historian Professor Robinson, encouraged her to apply to do a PhD with him on Benedictine monasteries of southern France, she was flattered, and then thrilled when she was awarded a Funding Council grant to carry out the research.

Points for Consideration

- Are new PhD students prepared for the difference in lifestyle as a postgraduate?
- Should this aspect be covered during the application process?

Becky spent the first six months of her research project reading voraciously and had started a course in Latin to enable her to read the source materials essential for her research. She had regular supervisory meetings with Professor Robinson who was impressed with the progress of her preliminary reading and gave favourable feedback on an initial draft of the first part of her literature review. But as the winter dragged on, she found that she was not nearly as happy as she felt she ought to be; after all she was working with one of the best minds in her field and he thought she was doing well. What could be wrong?

Point for Consideration

- Where is pastoral oversight of research students best catered for?

The problem was that Becky was lonely. Her friends had graduated and gone their separate ways and although one of her classmates, Emma, was also doing a PhD, she was in London. There were other PhD students in her department, but they were working in fields very different from her own. The students in the Latin class were all first-year undergraduates and she felt very old in comparison with them. She was sharing a house with a group of overseas students who tended to socialize with people from their own country. Professor Robinson had been very kind; he and his wife had invited Becky to dinner in the first month of her research. However, they were in their late fifties (older than Becky's parents) and had no children of their own. The dinner party had actually been rather difficult as Becky was terrified of committing a social gaffe and going down in the estimation of the great man. This certainly was not going to be the source of a lively social life.

Points for Consideration

- Should research students be helped to form relationships with a new peer group?
- How can the departmental culture be made more congenial to postgraduate researchers?

Becky tried to compensate for her loneliness by working even harder. She would stay in the library until it closed, to avoid having to go home to a group of students all talking in a language she couldn't understand. In early April she decided she needed a treat and went down to London to spend a long weekend with Emma. Emma was really enjoying her research into modern German poetry and enthused about the critical theory reading group she was part of and the weekly gender studies seminars she attended. These events usually ended up with everyone going to the pub and carrying on lively debates over drinks or a meal. The inevitable comparison between her lot and Emma's fuelled Becky's loneliness.

Points for Consideration

- Are there any warning signs that students are feeling isolated?
- If so, what remedial action might be taken?

Back home, Becky had to prepare for her transfer panel. She knew she could write the 4,000-word essay on an aspect of her research competently, but was having difficulty presenting an outline of the thesis. The research could go in so many different directions; how could she choose the best one to pursue? Professor Robinson did not share her anxiety. He pointed out that certain directions could enable her to make a much greater contribution to original research, indeed, could even be ground-breaking, even though they were more risky. But, he said, he had confidence in her intellectual abilities; she had shown she could work hard, she should not be afraid to aim high. Becky felt obliged to live up to this high opinion of her and agreed to follow her supervisor's advice.

Point for Consideration

- In what ways should supervisors take account of research students' inexperience as researchers?

In order to take her research further in this direction, Becky needed to visit an important archive in Toulors. She spent a frustrating few weeks trying to set up the visit and gain access to the necessary documents, but, despite references written by Professor Robinson, the staff were obstructive and unhelpful. Becky finally thought she had got the visit set up, but when she arrived in Toulors she was told that half of the records she wanted had been sent for conservation work. Nobody could tell her how long this would take; she would need to get in touch in 12–18 months time to see what the situation was. Becky was in despair, as she could afford neither the time nor the money for a return trip in a year or two's time.

Point for Consideration

- What contingency measures might be put in place if the student's research depends upon the cooperation of institutions beyond his/her control?

This setback was the final straw for Becky. She felt she had failed completely with the project and wanted nothing more to do with it. She could not bear the thought of going back to Professor Robinson and admitting she had let him down, so she went home to her parents. Becky now had time to sit and think about the situation. She concluded that she did not have the mental strength to cope with the isolation she experienced in the department nor with the sense of responsibility she felt regarding the successful completion of the research project. She doubted that she had what it took to devote herself to research in the way eminent academics such as Professor Robinson must do. She sat down and wrote a letter to the Head of Department, withdrawing from her PhD.

Points for Consideration

- How do we prepare research students for setbacks in the research process?
- Can we be sure that they have realistic expectations about what can or should be achieved?

Unsurprisingly, the Head of Department was taken completely aback when he received Becky's letter. All the records showed that she was a model student who was making excellent progress. When he consulted the student's supervisor, Professor Robinson was as puzzled as he was. The Head of Department asked the Graduate Tutor to convene a meeting of the departmental Graduate Research Committee, anxious not to lose a good student, nor the studentship she had been awarded. The Committee decided that Dr Smith, who had been Becky's personal tutor when she was an undergraduate student, should contact her to try to find out more about what lay behind her decision.

Point for Consideration

- How might involvement of other members of a department enhance the research student's experience?

Dr Smith managed to persuade Becky to come in and talk to him. At his prompting and with his support, Becky agreed to tell Professor Robinson about the disaster in Toulors. To Becky's surprise, Professor Robinson took this setback in his stride and was able to find plenty of salvageable material in the research she had already done. Two years later, Becky successfully completed and submitted her thesis. While it did not represent the ground-breaking research she had hoped for, she produced what the External Examiner considered a 'very worthy piece of work'.

Becky was happy with the outcome; however, when Professor Robinson suggested she should start to apply for research posts, Becky felt she needed to think carefully about whether she wanted to pursue an academic career. In many ways, the experience of the PhD deterred her; what she did know was that her decision must be based on an understanding of what research involved, not on another person's notion of what she should do.

Points for Consideration

- Are some personality types more suited to research than others?
- Should any account be taken of this in accepting students for research degrees?

Evolution of the problem

Although the student was not alone in the department, she was the only one working in her research area.

It is apparent that the student was unclear of whether anyone other than her supervisor in the department could help her situation.

Possible prevention and resolution of the problem

1. In disciplines where research is an individual, rather than a group, undertaking, departments need to consider measures to ensure that research students experience a congenial research culture and develop networks with their peers.
2. Students should be made to feel comfortable about seeking pastoral advice other than from their supervisor by contacting a second supervisor and/or the Graduate Tutor.
3. Eminent academics, in particular, should not lose sight of how students may look up to them which will lessen a student's willingness to report on lack of progress. Unfortunately, if this is the case, much bigger problems may emerge later on.

2

An Issue of Conflict

Scenario

Dr Landers, a mid-fifties, hard-working Senior Lecturer of some years standing, was desperate to get a Chair in Human Resource Management at Robert Jones University. While expanding her research team in support of her goal, she offered a PhD place to Alec, a promising new graduate and predicted high-flyer who had just gained a good first-class degree and was keen and excited to undertake some original research in the field of Human Resource Management. Alec eagerly accepted the position but at his first meeting with Dr Landers found her a little edgy, preoccupied, unforthcoming and somewhat sharp with him under the circumstances. However, he thought nothing more about it as he was already looking forward to focusing on his research, and starting work on the challenging and intriguing project that had been outlined to him.

Points for Consideration

- How important is the initial meeting between a supervisor and a student?
- What can be achieved at the initial meeting by the supervisor, on the one hand, and the student, on the other?
- Does a fairly superficial interaction between the supervisor and the student at an initial meeting represent a wasted opportunity for the supervisor?

About four weeks later, Dr Landers arranged a meeting with Alec, to discuss the minutiae and details of the strategy for progressing the early stages of the research project. The meeting got off to a bad start. Dr Landers was in a bad mood (she had just heard that her latest paper had been rejected by a top quality journal). She was further irritated, as Alec turned up late, as he had been 'talking to a friend' and forgot about the time. Dr Landers informed Alec in no uncertain terms what she thought about his tardiness, saying she hadn't time to waste waiting for him to turn up whenever he felt like it. Although the meeting proved useful to Alec, Dr Landers remained angry throughout, and at the end of the meeting instructed Alec to write a detailed review of the proposed research they had been discussing and submit it to her in a week's time. She would have a chance to read it and to work on it while travelling to a conference the following week. Alec worked hard at the review, and all was going well until he received an unexpected invitation to a friend's 21st party, which, as luck would have it, was some distance from the university. However, Alec had no intention of missing out on a good time so without telling anyone, and without handing in his nearly completed review, he went off to attend the party.

Points for Consideration

- Is it important that students become aware of the tight working timetable that busy supervisors have, of the importance of time management and of the imposition of deadlines for the completion of specific tasks?
- To what extent should a supervisor explain to a student the reasoning behind the setting of a deadline?
- Is it important for a student to try and understand the *modus operandi* and idiosyncrasies of their supervisor?

By the time Alec returned to the university, Dr Landers was away at the conference and he realized that assessment of his research review, with which he was very pleased, would have to wait until his supervisor's return. However, when Alec eventually met Dr Landers, he was somewhat surprised to find that she was very annoyed with him, informing him in no uncertain terms that she should have been told about his sudden absence without notice, and also that he would be late with his review. After this experience, Alec completed his review quickly, but on handing it to Dr Landers was dismayed to see her casually, almost, it seemed to Alec, disparagingly, throw it onto a huge pile of papers sitting in her in-tray, saying she was busy, it would now have to wait its turn, and that she would look at it when she had some time. What made matters seem worse to Alec, was that all these comments and actions were made in the presence of a second-year, female PhD student present in Dr Landers's office when Alec called to hand in his review.

Points for Consideration

- Do you consider the behaviour and actions of the student irresponsible?
- Are the attitude, behaviour and actions of the supervisor wise?
- How might the contretemps between supervisor and student have been avoided?

On thinking back, Alec became increasingly annoyed at Dr Landers. Maybe he had been a bit late with the review, but surely its importance and the thought and work he had put into it didn't warrant its being placed on the 'back burner' while he kicked his heels waiting to commence his research programme. As for his absence, surely he should be considered an adult now and could behave as he wanted. Why couldn't he take a few days off now and again without having to inform all and sundry? After a few days of seeing Dr Landers in the department, Alec formed the opinion that she was deliberately ignoring him and wondered what he should do next. He decided that he could start work on one particular aspect of his proposed research programme, that was outlined in his review, but it seemed that to do so in the most effective way, he would need Dr Landers's opinion on a few points of detail. Deciding to take the bull by the horns, Alec therefore went to arrange a meeting with Dr Landers. Although she seemed a bit sharp with him at first, she agreed to a meeting the following day.

Points for Consideration

- How do graduate students actually embark on their research studies, and how is the point at which they commence their work determined?
- Is the student's train of thought helpful to the developing situation?
- Can a student make the decision to commence research studies without the informed guidance and the say-so of the supervisor?

At the precise time of the pre-arranged meeting, Alec knocked on his supervisor's door but received no reply, although he could hear Dr Landers talking inside the room. On listening further, Alec realized that his supervisor was on the phone and decided to wait until she had finished her call. However, the conversation was still continuing 20 minutes later, so Alec decided to go off to do some further library work. When Dr Landers had finished the conversation, an extremely important call from her American collaborator, she looked for Alec, and was incensed to discover that he wasn't around.

Later in the day, just before Alec was about to go home, he saw his supervisor outside her office talking to a colleague, and decided he would ask if she had forgotten their meeting arranged for earlier in the day. Dr Landers couldn't believe what Alec was saying. She told him she had been waiting for him and that as he knew she was on the phone, he should have waited until she had finished. She went even further and said that as he was making a habit of not turning up for meetings, she would report him to the Head of Department. Alec reacted by saying that as she was so unreasonable to work with, he would report her to the Student's Union. Not surprisingly, no further meetings were arranged for a while.

> **Points for Consideration**
>
> - Should supervisors expect students to wait around until they are ready to see them?
> - Could the student have handled this situation in a more appropriate, tactful and helpful way?
> - At the commencement of a research programme and in establishing a working relationship, is it wise to maintain the student–supervisor contact at a formal level?
> - Why might both the supervisor and the student be over-reacting here?

Evolution of the problem

The decision placing a particular student with a particular supervisor will usually be made on purely academic grounds. While this will normally be acceptable and would be considered the optimal arrangement, there may occasionally be mismatches of personality.

The early enthusiasm of a student represents an extremely valuable platform for a supervisor to build on, and in this instance the supervisor either did not recognize, or else failed to consider, the initial keenness of the student. This represents a missed opportunity for the supervisor to establish a good working relationship with the student.

Keeping appointments and not being late are just as important for students as they are for staff. It is not surprising that the supervisor was angry when the student was late for a meeting, especially one in the early stages of the research programme that could be of considerable importance.

As the student had agreed to submit the review by a certain date, he should have kept to it. If he was going to give the review in late, then he should have informed his supervisor of this, along with a valid reason for the delay. In fact, the student did not have a valid reason, and was in the wrong for not informing the supervisor of the situation as a matter of courtesy.

Even though the supervisor had reason to be angry with the student, her actions on receiving the student's review could be construed as unreasonable, unprofessional and counterproductive. There is a lack of mutual respect, so important in establishing a working relationship.

Both supervisor and student appear unable to act courteously to one another, or to compromise with each other's failings. Both supervisor and student were aggravating the situation by their threats and counter-threats. Personality clashes and lack of respect can result in bizarre and unsympathetic reactions between individuals.

Possible prevention and resolution of the problem

1. Little attention is paid to personalities when matching a supervisor and student. While normally this will not be a problem, there will occasionally be mismatches of personality and the scenario will usually be obvious to the individuals concerned, but may be missed in the absence of rigorous student selection processes, or if the student is accepted by the supervisor for the wrong reasons.

2. Supervisors should take personal references seriously and preferably discuss suitability of student applicants with the referees. Students should, if possible, speak to present or former students of supervisors to be pre-warned of any foibles.

3. Like any working relationship, that between a supervisor and student needs time to develop and there has to be some give and take on both sides, especially in the early stages.

4. It is essential to establish the formal or informal nature of the contact between the supervisor and student, as well as the frequency of such contact, at the outset of the research programme.

5. Some appreciation by the student of a supervisor's working situation and patterns of behaviour may help in establishing and maintaining a good working relationship, and help the student realize the importance of both the concept and practice of effective time management.

6. It is a fair expectation that a student will attend pre-arranged meetings on time, and that such meetings will not be disrupted by telephone calls by or to the supervisor, or by other interruptions.

7. Graduate students, although relatively inexperienced, are adults, and should be treated as such. More reasonable and acceptable behaviour, based on mutual respect, by both supervisor and student is to be expected.

8. If supervisor–student personality clashes arise, a third party, a co-supervisor, or the departmental Graduate Tutor should be involved.

9. In some situations, the relationship may develop so badly that it may be thought irretrievable. If recognized early enough, the best option may be to change the supervisor.

3

An Issue of Non-Compliance

Scenario

Bernard had always been a strongly independent and imaginative character and it therefore came as something of a surprise to those who knew him to see him as a new PhD student in the highly successful research team of Professor Good, who worked on Prosthetic Joint research which was funded by major research council grants, and was generally regarded as a 'difficult' person to work for. At their first research meeting, Bernard had been a little taken aback as Professor Good had told him exactly what research work he would be doing and also how he would be doing it. Bernard's idea on how research should be undertaken was a little different from this. He believed that as a PhD student working in a high-powered team in a research-driven university, he would have the freedom to work, within his chosen field, on those topics that were of the greatest interest to him. His high level of self-confidence also allowed him to feel that, even with minimum input from his supervisor, he possessed enough imagination and ability to identify the core of a research problem in his area of interest, and sufficient knowledge to be able to select the direction of his research and the expertise which could provide him with the greatest chance of solving the problem. When all was said and done, it was his PhD and his future career.

Points for Consideration

- Could student independence of thought and action at an early stage in a research programme be less than beneficial to the student–supervisor relationship?
- At what stage in a research programme might a supervisor seek independence in their research students?
- How might headstrong students be discouraged in a tactful way?
- Can overconfidence be a source of contention and difficulty in the early stages of a research programme?

- Could the student be more helpful in establishing a relationship with the supervisor, and if so, in what way?

Like all staff and students in Professor Good's group, Bernard was expected to attend weekly research meetings, always held at 9.00 a.m. on a Monday morning, and to occasionally present progress on his work. However, Bernard had never considered himself an early riser, and, after an initial show of compliance, more often than not, failed to put in an appearance at these meetings. Understandably, Professor Good was not very happy about this. She could not conceive how anyone commencing a career in research could miss invaluable events for the group. Perhaps not surprisingly, she interpreted Bernard's behaviour as irresponsible and a failure to commit to both the work of the group, and to his own potential research future. For his part, Bernard was not too concerned, as he believed he was making some useful initial progress, even though he was taking little cognisance of Professor Good's e-mailed directives and instructions.

Points for Consideration

- How may a student's progress be optimally assessed?
- Is this achieved at one-to-one meetings with a supervisor, or are other formats of equal value for the purpose?
- Should the progress of all students be assessed by similar means, or is there room for different approaches, dependent on the character of the student?

It was about five months into the project when Professor Good decided it was time she told Bernard to toe the line. At their meeting, Professor Good told Bernard that although she felt he had made some progress overall, he was deviating somewhat from the project he was 'signed up' to, and that the funding for his project was to investigate a well-defined and specific area of research. Even if he were to uncover an interesting research line to follow, she, and indeed all the members of the team, should be made aware of this. It could lead to future funding opportunities for the group, but with Bernard's relative lack of experience, she was the one who was in a position to make a judgement on the findings and possessed the 'know-how' to chase the funding for them, should that be appropriate. She also indicated to Bernard that she would be grateful if he could attend those very important research group meetings so everyone would be aware of his current progress, and also, of course, his contribution to the group overall. She added, finally, that if Bernard could make just a little more effort to do what he had been selected to do, as well as to act more as a member of the team, then she thought all would be well and his future would be looking good.

Points for Consideration

- Has the supervisor handled this situation acceptably?
- Should apparently outstanding, imaginative but perhaps headstrong research students, be allowed more leeway?
- Could the student interpret the situation as the supervisor taking advantage of student inexperience to appropriate ideas for her own future use?

Bernard was somewhat taken aback by Professor Good's comments. After all, he was no longer an undergraduate, he was now in his early twenties and considered that having some independence of thought and action was a reasonable expectation. However, he did not particularly want to upset Professor Good and therefore replied that he would try and do things properly in future.

Another three months went by and little had changed, despite Bernard's promises. Bernard was still rarely seen at the research group meetings and when Professor Good eventually got to meet him to discuss his work and his progress, he still seemed to be going off at a tangent and not really focusing on the principal research question with which he should be involved. Professor Good was very concerned. She could not allow Bernard to deviate further from the research for which she had received funding, and she had already had an earlier meeting with him in which she had put her views quite strongly. What was she to do? No matter how he performed in the transfer meeting, he would not be allowed to continue because she was fully pre-pared to make it clear to the transfer panel that this student was not focusing his research efforts on what he should be doing. Ideally, she would like to replace him before too much time was wasted but she realized that would not be possible at the present time.

Points for Consideration

- Is either the student or the supervisor acting unreasonably in this situation?
- Has the supervisor allowed sufficient time after their earlier meeting, for the student to change his ways?
- What impressions might the student be giving to his colleagues in the research group?
- Could the attitudes and behaviour of the research group be adversely affected by the student's approach to the team's research programme?
- Do you think the grounds on which the supervisor is basing the decision not to recommend transfer, are valid?

Evolution of the problem

A student has to want to be supervised. In this case, the student resists the advice of his supervisor, and the student's whole attitude to his research project is inappropriate for a new and junior member of the team.

In certain research areas, feedback on student progress is made in a group setting. Non-attendance at such meetings gives a bad impression, and could unsettle the group, particularly if the group thinks that the student is being given preferential treatment.

Despite the supervisor's tactful warning, the student made no attempt to change his ways and show any commitment to a team approach.

Many research topics are clearly defined and it is very important to concentrate activities towards the main theme; too much sidetracking is not only foolish but can be potentially damaging.

The apparently entrenched position and strong views of the student regarding the research environment and how research should be conducted, suggest he will not change, and he therefore represents something of a problem for the supervisor.

Possible prevention and resolution of the problem

1. An induction event, clearly outlining the responsibilities of both supervisor and student in the research environment leading to a higher degree, should help students understand what is expected of them, and what to expect in the student–supervisor working relationship.
2. The student could be asked to withdraw from the project and terminate his registration. If he could be made to see that in the long term this would not be damaging to his career, then this could be a viable option.
3. Should the student feel strongly that he has every right to continue, he should be reported to the Dean for lack of progress. As he has done little of what he should have done, his registration could well be terminated by the institution. If he were allowed one further chance, then conditions would have to be set to a specified timescale. If the student failed to meet these conditions, his registration would be terminated.
4. For the sake of the reputation of both the supervisor and the research team, a quick solution should be sought to allow remaining grant monies to be used to employ a more suitable replacement student.

4

An Issue of Plagiarism

Scenario

Although already supervising two home-based students, Astrid, from a small, developing Eastern European country, was the first overseas student assigned to, and accepted by Dr Neville James, a young member of staff in the Department of Statistics at Humbleton University. Astrid, a personable and attractive young lady, had made a good impression on Dr James at their initial interview. She seemed highly motivated, with an apparently good background knowledge of the research topics that interested Dr James, as far as he could gather, although her spoken English left something to be desired. However, she possessed references and qualifications deemed to be roughly equivalent to those obtained in the UK, and had attained an acceptable TOEFL score of 550. She also knew all about Dr James's research publications. After interviewing her, Dr James discussed Astrid with the department's Graduate Tutor, and it was agreed between them that she should be offered an MPhil/PhD place in the department.

Points for Consideration

- How might this student, borderline on paper, have been further assessed?
- Why might this interview have been conducted with less than adequate probing and with insufficient depth?
- How much weight should be given to non-standard qualifications in making the appointment of an overseas student?

At the commencement of the semester, Dr James requested Astrid to produce a comprehensive literature review of relevance to the research project they had agreed she should pursue. They discussed and selected the Research Training Programme (RTP) modules that she should take during her first year, and he set Astrid to work in the Graduate Student research room on the agreed research topic. The semester proved a hectic one for Dr James. The mountain of paper he was asked to supply for the Subject Teaching Programme Review kept growing almost to the day the Review took place; in addition, that year the department had taken on an increased number of undergraduates, and had lost three academic staff members to early retirement, as a result of which, Dr James became embroiled in extra teaching work. Nevertheless, he managed to keep up his research meetings throughout the semester with each of his three graduate students individually, although some of the meetings were necessarily somewhat brief and cursory.

Points for Consideration

- What priority should a supervisor give to the needs of a newly-appointed graduate student commencing their research studies?
- Can the work and time devoted to the RTP modules provide an unwanted distraction at the commencement of a research programme?

Late in January, Astrid produced both her draft literature review and a report on her research progress to date. Both pieces of work were somewhat overlong, repetitive in places, but Dr James thought, pleasantly surprising for a first-year overseas graduate student, as they were well written in good English, well constructed, word-processed and easy to deal with. Dr James was able to read through them rapidly and return both pieces of work to Astrid within a few days, accompanied by some minor comments, but including a particular one commending Astrid on her good command of written English.

Point for Consideration

- How might a supervisor miss evidence of student plagiarism, and how easy is it to detect evidence of such plagiarism in literature reviews and research reports?

About a month later, Dr James had a research meeting with Astrid to discuss her review and report, and his comments on, and interpretation of her work. Rather surprisingly he found the discussion to be somewhat one-sided, consisting mainly of Dr James elaborating on the points he was making regarding her work, suggesting possible research directions she might profitably wish to follow, but with very little input from Astrid herself. However, she seemed a good listener, taking it all in, and appeared to be in complete agreement with all of Dr James's proposals.

> ## Points for Consideration
>
> - What might be the reasons for the lack of adequate responses from the student?
> - Does the lack of response from the student indicate her failure to engage with the research topic?
> - How can a supervisor establish a relationship with a student that is of sufficient depth to expose possible student shortcomings?
> - What might the lack of concordance between the student's written work and her lack of verbal communication with the supervisor imply?

Two further pieces of work were received by Dr James during the second semester, the latter with accompanying information from Astrid to the effect that she had successfully completed three RTP modules. It appeared to Dr James that Astrid was proving an industrious student, although perhaps lacking insight as both pieces of submitted work gave little indication of progress along the research directions they had discussed earlier. Indeed, although well written (but showing rather alarming evidence of Americanization), Astrid's reports consisted, more or less, of rehashed reviews of the overall aims of the topic, and Dr James felt uneasy about them. If Astrid had gained a good grasp of the overall aims of her research project, why was her subsequent progress less than satisfactory? She seemed a hard worker, he had had sufficient contact with her, and although somewhat uncommunicative since their early meetings, he could have sworn she would have coped admirably with her research project.

Early in May, Dr James had occasion to re-read a recent electronic publication stemming from a highly respected group based in Arizona, who were working on an aspect of Statistical Probability that impinged on Astrid's research topic, and was amazed to find himself reading, not quite verbatim, but pretty much so, a number of paragraphs that might have been lifted directly from one of Astrid's research progress reports! It was immediately clear to him that he was facing a possible case of plagiarism and he hurried back to his office armed with the American group's publication to carefully sift through Astrid's two most recent research reports. There was no doubt; almost half of one of them, and one-third of the second, contained elements extracted from the American publication, and although there had been some modifications and substitutions of individual words together with some changes in paragraph order, the sentence construction and the phraseology as well as the conclusions that were drawn in each section of Astrid's reports where the plagiarized material appeared, closely followed the lay-out of the American document.

Points for Consideration

- How can the distinction between plagiarism and the genuine use of other people's work as supportive evidence be made?
- How might the supervisor confirm his suspicions of plagiarism?
- What reason might a research student have for indulging in plagiarism?

It so happened that the first-year presentations were due to take place in about three weeks, and Dr James decided to see how Astrid performed in her talk before taking any further steps; after all, this was still quite early days in her graduate student work, and he could be doing her an injustice. Accordingly, he e-mailed Astrid saying he was too busy to see her about her reports, but he would be attending her presentation. However, Dr James decided to carefully examine all the earlier written work he had received from Astrid and here also he unearthed further evidence of plagiarism, although not to quite the same extent as he had found in her most recent written work.

Points for Consideration

- Is the supervisor's decision to hold fire on any action and to confirm his suspicions a good one?
- Should anyone else be consulted and brought into the picture at this stage?
- How should the student be approached with regard to her plagiarism?

At the presentations, Astrid was the penultimate student to speak, and it was quite clear to Dr James (and to the other academic members of staff present), that Astrid was having considerable difficulties with her research work. Besides being hesitant, disjointed, superficial, unfocused, and lacking in confidence, her talk consisted primarily of a rehash of her earlier literature review, and there was little evidence in the presentation that she was either aware of, or had progressed, down even the clearest of research lines that might take her project forward, although, as Dr James well knew, she had read at least something of the work of other groups in the field! Although the audience remained as supportive as possible throughout her talk, it was obvious to everyone, including Astrid herself, that this was not a good performance, even allowing for her lack of fluency in English, that her shortcomings in research capability had been brutally exposed. This was particularly apparent with her poor handling of the questions she received at the end of her talk. Dr James had some hard thinking and hard talking to do, and some difficult decisions to make.

Evolution of the problem

Inadequacies in the student selection procedures have not helped this problem, and there was only limited consultation by the prospective supervisor with other, probably more experienced, academic staff members, including the departmental Graduate Tutor, both at the time of selection and throughout the development of the problem. The supervisor may have been unaware that some students, to maximize their chances of selection, may target the work of a prospective supervisor, and spend time learning the nature of the research interests of the supervisor, maximizing their chances of a successful interview.

The student was probably not up to the job of undertaking research work, but this was not detected at the time of selection as her capabilities for research were not adequately explored. The English language capabilities of the student also were not investigated thoroughly enough at the time of selection.

The workload of the supervisor at the commencement of the student's research project may have precluded the early arousal of supervisor suspicions of a potential problem, in that there was no time for detailed, in-depth, probing discussions with the student or for the supervisor to make time for a comprehensive examination of the student's research reports. As a result, the supervisor might have missed evidence of student plagiarism.

Concentration on the RTP modules might have represented a relatively easy option for the student, and provide a useful distraction, rather than spending all her available time trying to come to grips with the greater demands of her research programme.

The supervisor's decision to postpone any action, until after the student presentation, although allowing the garnering of supportive evidence for the problem of student competence and evidence of plagiarism, exacerbated the problem, and brought the situation into the public domain in a way that can be less than helpful for its smooth resolution.

Possible prevention and resolution of the problem

1. In-depth and enlightened use of appropriate graduate student selection procedures must be in place, particularly for applicants with a 'non-standard' background. Following an interview, should a supervisor, for whatever reason, harbour doubts about the suitability of a prospective graduate student to carry out research work, then it is advisable to arrange for the student to be seen by another, preferably more experienced member of staff, or by the department's Graduate Tutor.
2. A more searching assessment of overseas student quality and capabilities at the application stage, preferably in the student's home country, will help to avoid the inadvertent selection of a student unsuited for research work.

3. Graduate students embarking on a programme of research work should be advised of the importance, nature and relevance of plagiarism to the research work setting, ideally as part of a Graduate Student Induction Course. Students should also be aware that computer software is available to supervisors to check for plagiarism in electronic documents and that it is being increasingly used.

4. Close supervision should be given to all students at the outset of their research programme, and especially to those for whom English is not their first language. The supervisor should prioritize his workload to ensure student needs are understood and met at the commencement of their research programme, and that an effective and open working relationship between student and supervisor is established early on.

5. There should also be careful prioritization of the first year's work of the student under the guidance of the supervisor, and this should take into consideration the relative time the student allots to the RTP modules and to establishing an ongoing research programme.

6. Earlier realization by the supervisor that a problem might exist, and earlier involvement of other, more experienced, academic staff members and the Graduate Tutor, might have led to a more positive resolution to the problem.

7. A decision on whether the student continues with her research studies (with the same or a different supervisor), or whether she be recommended to transfer to a PhD, or be asked to leave in view of the plagiarism and/or on the basis of lack of clear research ability, will depend on a thorough reassessment of the student's capabilities and on the reasons for her plagiarism. Advice should be taken on whether formal procedures for dealing with allegations of plagiarism should be invoked. The transfer step can serve to provide an official stage at which such decisions can be formalized.

5

An Issue of Time

Scenario

Although Aubrey Lister had not done any academic work since he gained his first degree ten years previously, he was very keen to study for a research degree, as there was no doubt that he regarded a widened knowledge and understanding of the subject of Consultative Management of Small Businesses to be an extremely useful and most appropriate adjunct to his professional career. Aubrey was currently working in middle management, and for his third company over a working period of about ten years, and had decided to study a particular area of relevant research on a part-time basis rather than take a more general MBA. He had therefore contacted his local university looking for an academic who would both want, and be able, to supervise his research in his specific area of interest. Fortunately, Dr Stocks, a member of the university staff, who appeared to Aubrey to have the correct background, and who was heavily involved in private consultancy work through his university department, replied very positively to Aubrey's query.

Point for Consideration

- Unlike some new graduates who move into research immediately following graduation and who may do so simply because the opportunity comes their way, part-time students tend to be well-motivated, career-orientated and desperately keen to study.

Once Aubrey had registered for his higher degree, Dr Stocks arranged to have a meeting with him at a local wine bar, in order to plan the most appropriate approach to the proposed research and discuss any other interests they might have in common, and that could be of use to either of them. Dr Stocks found Aubrey to be a charming character working, what's more, for a company that might well have applications that impinged on some aspects of his own private research work. The meeting turned out to be a very pleasant occasion, and Aubrey and Dr Stocks seemed to get along swimmingly. Aubrey left the meeting feeling very pleased in several ways, but most particularly about the research proposals and the project that he and Dr Stocks had put together. In addition, Dr Stocks had been able to reassure Aubrey he would have plenty of time to complete his PhD as the time limit for part-time students was twice that for full-time students. For example, it would probably be at least two years, or even longer before Aubrey would need to think about his transfer from the MPhil to the PhD programme.

Points for Consideration

- With people leading busy lives, and often working long hours, part-time research students must be fully aware of the time commitment they must make.
- Would you expect the quality of a part-time MPhil/PhD programme to be equivalent to that of a full-time one, and if not, why not?
- Are the student's initial enthusiasm and motivation sufficiently supported by the supervisor?
- How might the supervisor provide more support for the student?

A few months went by before Dr Stocks, who had come across an intriguing new development which might have relevance to Aubrey's research, gave any more thought to either his part-time student or to the research project they were involved in. His realization that he had not attempted to contact Aubrey since their initial meeting caused Dr Stocks some slight pangs of guilt, but these were speedily assuaged when he considered that Aubrey, for his part, had failed to make contact with him. He therefore decided to e-mail Aubrey there and then to see how his research was progressing. It just so happened that Aubrey was away on company business at the time, and it was a few days before Dr Stocks got a reply to the effect that the last few weeks had been rather busy ones for Aubrey as he had been involved in trying to secure an overseas contract for his company, and as a consequence, had had little time to think about anything else. He had thus made hardly any progress on his research project. Nevertheless, he informed Dr Stocks, the contract for his company had been successfully negotiated, and he felt certain he would now get more time to spend on the literature review that he urgently needed to complete, and give some attention to the initial aspects of his research programme.

Points for Consideration

- With whom, supervisor or student, does the onus of responsibility for making contact lie?

- What contact should there be between the graduate student, the supervisor and the student's employers?
- When should such contact take place?
- How may part-time students be encouraged to attend departmental induction events?
- Should mature, busy, part-time students be expected to attend departmental seminars and research talks?

Several more months elapsed and Aubrey thought it was about time he should meet his supervisor to update him as to the progress he had made and what his current situation was. Fortunately, Aubrey had not been quite so busy at work and had had the time to complete his literature review. However, this had not proved quite so simple, and Aubrey's progress had been frustrated as the University Library's restricted opening times in the evenings and at weekends, proved a major problem for him as these were really the only times he was free to access the library. Eventually, almost in desperation, he had been forced to miss time with his young family on several Saturday mornings to give himself a chance to get to the library. In spite of Aubrey's concerns about his progress, however, the meeting with his supervisor proved to be a very congenial one. Dr Stocks was very interested in the 'goings on' at Aubrey's company, appeared pleased with the progress Aubrey had managed to achieve with his literature review, and encouraged him to move it forward as speedily as possible, and to 'ease his way' into his research programme proper.

About 18 months after Aubrey had registered for his MPhil/PhD, Dr Stocks suddenly realized that it was time to be thinking about Aubrey's transfer to PhD, and consequently, through e-mail, attempted to arrange a further meeting with his student. Once again Dr Stocks did not receive an immediate reply from Aubrey, but when, eventually, he did obtain a response, he was taken aback to hear that Aubrey's company had been taken over by a much larger business enterprise from the USA. As Aubrey relayed the details of this takeover to Dr Stocks at their meeting, it was clear that apart from Aubrey's concerns about his own future at the new company, he was also concerned that his research might well now be in jeopardy; the small business Aubrey had originally joined had grown into a much larger concern, and there would almost certainly be priority changes inspired by the takeover. This meeting was not such a happy one as the previous one, as Dr Stocks came to realize that Aubrey had a number of real difficulties. For one thing, Aubrey could not see how he would be able to continue with his research project in his new circumstances, while Dr Stocks, for a number of reasons of his own, felt somewhat relieved that his part-time researcher, and his research project might now have to be shelved. Accordingly, at the end of their discussions, he suggested to Aubrey that possibly the best option for all concerned would be for Aubrey to withdraw his MPhil/PhD registration.

> ### Points for Consideration
>
> • At what point in time should a supervisor (and the student) begin to consider, and plan for, the transfer process?
>
> • How might unforeseen eventualities such as a company takeover, a potential hazard in these situations, be guarded against?
>
> • Is the supervisor acting in everyone's best interests in withdrawing his support at the first major sign of trouble or is he being realistic?

Evolution of the problem

Even though a mature student, the student did not think carefully enough of the time commitment that would be involved in his part-time research study, in view of his demanding job, access to the university facilities, possible changes in his work schedule and ease of contact with his supervisor.

No consultation between the student, his employers and the supervisor took place to discuss the management of the student and his research programme prior to commencement of the research work, or during its early stages.

The supervisor was unwise in telling the student that as time limits for part-time research degrees were substantially longer than for full-time degrees, he would have plenty of time, without at least qualifying the statement with regard to the possible pitfalls and problems that can arise during a research project.

No organized meetings schedule with the student was set up by the supervisor. When meetings did occur, they were haphazard and infrequent, apparently occurring only when either student or supervisor felt too much time had elapsed since their previous contact.

The supervisor's motives for taking on the student were questionable. He may have been more interested in the possible contacts and links that he might be able to establish with the company employing the student.

There was no planning or preparation made by the supervisor, on behalf of the student, for the transfer process, and to be unprepared for this situation is a result of bad research time management. This was exacerbated by the supervisor's indications to the student that, as a part-time student, he would have ample time to complete his research.

When major and unpredictable events at work occur, usually beyond the control of the student, they may seriously affect the student's ability to study and progress the research. When an individual, already in long-term employment, wishes to undertake part-time study leading to an MPhil/PhD research degree, it implies considerable dedication and commitment in both time and hard work on the part of that individual. The supervisor failed to respond in any positive way to the student's predicament, and did not provide the student with any support from which he might possibly benefit. Indeed, if that is what he wanted, the supervisor had been provided with an excuse to terminate the project, and his 'contract' with the student which had not been going smoothly.

Possible prevention and resolution of the problem

1. When part-time students are seriously considering an application to study for a research degree, they should have a preliminary meeting with the Head of Department or the departmental Graduate Tutor, so that they can be made aware of particular difficulties associated with this mode of study.
2. The employers of a part-time research student must, of course, be fully aware of the student's proposed undertaking, and should ideally give the student and his or her research programme their full support. Ideally also, the employers of the prospective student should be brought into discussions surrounding the research project and its management at some point early in the proceedings.
3. The concept of managing research time and the scheduling of supervisory meetings should have been discussed in detail at the initial meeting between the supervisor and the student. At the same time, the supervisor could have made the point that part-time students can often feel isolated from the mainstream activities, and from their peers and colleagues in the department to which they are attached, simply through the nature of their situation. Although electronic mail may help in lessening the feeling of isolation, it is important that supervisors appreciate this potential problem and can respond accordingly, ensuring the student is kept informed of, and at least invited to attend, seminars, meetings and any functions the department may organize.
4. Institutions and departments need to seriously consider, and to have in place if not already there, adequate provision to meet the needs of part-time research students.
5. To be more positive and helpful towards his student's difficult situation, in discussions with the student, the supervisor could have given consideration to, and if possible, proposed some alternative or slightly modified way of looking at the student's original research programme, which might have provided the student with an opportunity to discuss with his employers at least the possibility of continuing his research.

6

An Issue of Language

Scenario

A new doctoral programme had been introduced in the Department of Architectural Studies at Stocksbury University, and Dr Eddie Williams was pleased to have the chance of attracting a number of graduate students, to help give the department a useful research boost. Unfortunately, the marketing of the new programme had been left rather late and there were fewer applications than expected. However, one applicant from overseas, Anna Afham, seemed very keen to join the new doctoral programme, and sent several e-mails to Dr Williams requesting further details and information. Encouraged by this, Dr Williams hoped that once Anna's application had been received, an offer to her could be made fairly quickly.

> ### Points for Consideration
> - Is there any value in a supervisor keeping in touch with a prospective student making preparations to join a research programme at a UK university?
> - How might a supervisor ascertain the suitability of a prospective overseas graduate student for a research degree?

However, when Anna's application finally arrived, there was a problem. Her TOEFL score was only 530 and the minimum requirement for overseas graduate student entry to the course was 550. Dr Williams was initially disappointed by this but then considered that Anna's e-mails seemed well written, suggesting he could probably cope with her English if she proved as enthusiastic for the research programme as she sounded, and anyway, could he afford not to receive the overseas student funding that she would bring with her? Following discussions with the department admissions tutor, it was agreed that, just to be sure, he would interview her by telephone. This was a good idea in theory, but after several frustrating experiences of either getting cut-off or lines going dead, Dr Williams realized that if he did not accept her soon, Anna's funding would not be available to him in time for the start of the new programme. So an offer was duly made, and Anna arrived just in time to commence her studies.

Points for Consideration

- Is the supervisor wise in ignoring the student's TOEFL score?
- What should be the role of the departmental admissions tutor in such cases?
- Is the supervisor justified in accepting the student based on his perception of her e-mails?
- Is he right to accept the student without interview?
- To what extent should the availability of funding be a factor in determining acceptance of an overseas student onto a research programme?

Dr Williams was of course pleased to see Anna who was visiting the UK for the first time, and had come over with her sister who was one year older than Anna. Anna's sister, who would be sharing accommodation with her, was also starting a PhD (in English literature) at the same university. At Anna's first meeting with Dr Williams, he noticed she did not say a great deal, but put it down to her being in a new country and new surroundings, being a little shy and perhaps somewhat overawed. At their subsequent meetings, however, Anna's behaviour remained unchanged, and it seemed to Dr Williams that although Anna was making every effort with her research studies, her competence in both spoken and written English was not nearly as good as he would have wished. Nevertheless, it was still early days and Dr Williams thought that once Anna had been in the country for a while and gained more experience in English, her language should improve considerably.

Points for Consideration

- Can the presence of close family influence the adaptation of students to their new surroundings and situation?
- At what points and by what means might the supervisor act to deal with potential language difficulties?
- What support should universities provide to overseas students with language difficulties?

As a conscientious supervisor, Dr Williams had regular meetings with Anna to monitor her research progress, and push her research programme along, and these arrangements had been quite acceptable until now. As time went by, however, Dr Williams realized that Anna's competence in English was showing little improvement. Her attempt at a literature review was really quite poor and Dr Williams began to wonder whether she would in fact be capable of writing a lucid and coherent report in support of her transfer without considerable assistance. As for the mini-*viva* which she would necessarily have to go through, he was quite worried that Anna would be unable to clearly communicate to the transfer panel that she understood the nature of her work, or indeed handle the searching questions that, no matter how gentle the panel might be, she would undoubtedly have to face. Eventually, and after much consideration, Dr Williams decided his best course of action would be to delay the transfer meeting, thereby allowing Anna more time to address her problems with the English language, that he felt was at the root of her difficulties.

Points for Consideration

- To what extent should a supervisor assist a student in writing a piece of work such as a transfer report?
- Is the supervisor acting in the best interests of the student in postponing the interview with the transfer panel?
- Has the supervisor established an effective working relationship with the student?
- What course of action might the supervisor be advised to follow?
- What independent action might be available to the student?

Anna herself, however, became very upset when she realized her transfer was to be delayed and began to worry that the delay might jeopardize her funding, casting an aspersion on her research abilities, and implying that she would be unable to successfully complete a PhD. Although Anna was aware her competence in English could be improved, her supervisor had never made a big issue of it before now. Unfortunately, neither Anna nor Dr Williams had any clear plans to improve the situation.

Evolution of the problem

Despite pressures on the supervisor, the student should not have been accepted with a TOEFL score of only 530. A requirement of 550 is still low and many departments are now raising the level of acceptance to 600 and above.

The supervisor should, perhaps, have tried to maintain more contact with the student during the months she spent in making preparations to come to the UK. Because of late applications from prospective overseas students, unacceptable pressures can be experienced by departments to accept students onto research degree programmes. Funding requirements were also a consideration in the acceptance of the student onto the new research programme.

The supervisor's decision to accept the student was made through focusing on the wrong reasons, and might even be seen as naïve. Although it may seen rather cynical, overseas applicants may not have actually written letters, faxes or e-mails themselves without assistance. (Could the applicant's sister have helped her with the application?) Also there is no way of knowing whether the person being interviewed by telephone is in fact the applicant.

It is not unusual for overseas students to bring their families with them. The disadvantage of this is that English is rarely spoken in the home and students with English-speaking difficulties will not be helped in this sort of environment.

The supervisor was aware that the student's language competence could be a problem, but arrangements for her to be thoroughly assessed and appropriately supported at an early stage in her studies were not made. The supervisor also failed to set up a sufficiently good working relationship with the student to enable him to communicate his views on both her language problems and her research abilities to help her through this difficult time.

The student was aware she had achieved a low TOEFL score and that she was responsible for improving this situation, which she failed to do.

Little assistance appears to have been provided to the student in writing either her literature review or her transfer report.

The supervisor's decision to delay the appearance of the student before the transfer panel, was, in the circumstances, probably the most appropriate course of action. However, the situation should not have been allowed to develop, and procrastination and avoidance of the problem may well create further, perhaps more serious difficulties, at a later date.

Continuation of funding can often depend on the progress of the student. A delay in the MPhil/PhD transfer might compromise the student's funding, and at the outset it is important for the supervisor to know the conditions of any scholarship, especially those from overseas.

There were no plans in place to help resolve the student's difficulties. Unless something was done, the transfer issue can only be a delaying tactic.

Possible prevention and resolution of the problem

1. Involvement of academic staff in the graduate student admissions process may help ensure that English language requirements for overseas students are adhered to. The assessment of the situation with regard to the quality and potential of overseas students in their home country is undertaken by some universities through visits to the countries, as well as through recent experience with graduates from the country concerned already studying in the UK.
2. There are advantages in a supervisor maintaining some contact with a prospective student from overseas who is making preparations to embark on a higher degree programme. Such contact can ensure the authenticity

of the prospective student's credentials and educative background, and also prepares the ground for the early establishment of a good working relationship between the supervisor and the student.

3. It would have been helpful to have asked the student to undergo further English language training and re-sit the TOEFL exam, so that an adequate score could be obtained. Alternatively, and if possible, the student could have been asked to come to the university several months early to undergo further English language training before the start of the research programme.

4. Graduate students may require considerable assistance from a supervisor with their writing in the early stages of their research work, and also at the stage of thesis write-up, and this may be particularly so for overseas students. Ideally, a supervisor should find time to help overseas students in particular, with the preparation and writing of the important transfer report. Such help also provides both supervisor and student with the opportunity to exchange information and understanding, and this may formulate the working relationship between the two. Ideally, assistance with writing should decrease with time and with the increasing experience of the student.

5. A supervisor may help a student in the early stages by requesting written assignments on aspects of the research or reviews of key references. In this way it is possible to get a better idea of whether the student has a problem with comprehension of the subject and/or difficulties with the English language. Asking students to give oral presentations may provide similar information and help the students' language problems.

6. If a supervisor suspects a student might be experiencing a problem with the English language, many universities have English Language Training Centres (ELTCs), where students can be fully assessed and recommendations made as to which areas of English language need improvement. Often, specific ELTC courses are free to registered students. A supervisor should take advantage of ELTCs and strongly encourage students to commit themselves fully to these courses.

7

An Issue of Writing

Mick Hattaway

Scenario

Geoffrey had done his first degree at the University of Loamshire and applied to do his PhD with Professor Foster as he was a recognized authority on English literature of the Early Modern Period. Geoffrey had been awarded a First (just!) and had received generally positive references that commended his diligence, thoroughness, ability to read widely and methodically, and enthusiasm for his chosen area of research.

Geoffrey proposed a PhD on the method of use of classical mythology in the plays of John Marston, a contemporary of Shakespeare. His work proceeded slowly because he had first to familiarize himself with aspects of the huge range of classical texts that would have been familiar to any young man living in the Early Modern Period who had successfully completed even a grammar school education (where the instruction would have been based on Latin).

Points for Consideration

- Might the student's application and references have been more thoroughly scrutinized before an offer of graduate study was made, and if so, how?
- Was the topic a viable one for an undergraduate with little knowledge of classical languages?

The instruction at the time would have assumed or involved some familiarity with rhetorical practice as well as with mythological handbooks that today are unknown, not having been translated from the original Latin or Italian. To help deal with his problem, Geoffrey did sign up for a one-year course in Latin, but that did not take him very far. Geoffrey also was required to read as voraciously as possible the drama of Marston's contemporaries, in order to evolve comparative perspectives that he could use to establish hypotheses concerning the 'methods of use'. He needed to find out about theatrical production methods, and the composition and nature of the coterie audiences for which Marston wrote. Finally, he needed to survey relevant secondary material and start work on an enumerative bibliography of the topic.

Point for Consideration

- Is the student receiving adequate support at this early stage of his research?

Professor Foster was well aware of the difficulties of finding academic employment without substantial publication, preferably a monograph, and always encouraged his students to conceive of their dissertations as 'books' rather than as 'theses' – the intention being to enable them to submit a manuscript to a publisher as soon as possible after gaining their PhD.

Point for Consideration

- Is the supervisor right to fuse research and employment considerations?

After some preliminary instruction, Geoffrey showed considerable skill in information retrieval; he made excellent use of EndNote Plus (a bibliographical programme) and soon amassed a seemingly comprehensive list of secondary sources. He also was able to search electronic archives, and produced impressive lists of quotations from Renaissance texts containing references to key figures such as Diana, Ganymede, the Satyrs, and so forth. However, his first piece of written work did not appear on time and the few generalizations it contained followed well-worn tracks and were embedded in excessively long lists of examples. His supervisor found it a dreary read, and, moreover, considered that Geoffrey was almost tone-deaf, not appreciative of the elements of wit, pastiche, and parody that are characteristic of Marston's writing.

Points for Consideration

- How might a student working away from centres like London and Stratford where, from time to time, productions of plays of relevance to him might be seen, gain the necessary experience to detect the subtleties of tone?
- Can a critical ear be trained?
- Are these 'subtleties' really demonstrable or open to analysis, or do they derive from the sensibilities of contemporary 'experts', who in turn construct a cultural moment or milieu for an author or playwright according to their own proclivities?
- To what extent, if at all, can and should the opinions, prejudices and interpretations of the supervisor, with respect to a body of work being researched, dictate or delineate the writing of the student?

After the first, rather unsatisfactory, piece of written work submitted at the end of the first semester, Professor Foster provided Geoffrey with some detailed notes on Marston's writing, and suggested that Geoffrey move on to look at another group of plays and gain wider understanding of the analysis of different kinds of Marstonian texts, both theatrical and non-theatrical, before revising his first effort. He also encouraged Geoffrey to write more, and more frequently, suggesting that a higher proportion of their supervisory sessions should be based on specific smaller-scale pieces of work written by Geoffrey. In this way, he hoped to help Geoffrey sharpen his awareness of verbal subtleties before producing the piece of work required for his transfer panel at the end of his first year's research. He also tentatively raised the question of developing a critical framework, mentioning the work of Jürgen Habermas.

Points for Consideration

- How does one define an appropriate context?
- Should it be inclusive of as many examples of a particular practice as possible, or should the student write in a more concentrated way on a smaller range of examples?
- Can the supervisor's knowledge and information about potential External Examiners for a PhD student, influence the mode, style and approach of the writing?
- Many academics demand that literacy criticism be infused by 'theory': how are theoretical approaches to be selected?

Geoffrey, however, spent a significant amount of time during the second semester of his first year revising his first piece of work rather than widening his analysis to include key passages from a larger range of plays. When he handed it in to Professor Foster, it was shorn of many examples and analogies but, in the supervisor's view, no more perceptive. Geoffrey had covered very little new ground before the summer vacation, but Professor Foster was somewhat reassured that his student had begun to read Habermas and, indeed, seemed to have been inspired by his ideas.

When a second major piece of written work eventually arrived, the balance between weight of material and critical treatment was much more satisfactory. Professor Foster had mused about the difficulties of building bridges between post-Marxist descriptions of social movements and post-structuralist concentrations on language, which is why he had tentatively suggested Habermas. However, over the long vacation, Geoffrey seemed to his supervisor to have turned into a disciple, and generated an essay in which all the analyses relentlessly used the categories of the German critic in a mechanical way. The essay's methodological superstructure seemed far too heavy for its base. Yet this was to be the piece of work Geoffrey was submitting for the end-of-year review in the autumn and was to be used to determine whether his registration be transferred to a PhD.

Points for Consideration

- Has there been sufficient dialogue between the supervisor and the student to assist the latter with his writing methodology?
- Is the supervisor expecting too much of the student?
- Should students be left, alone, effectively to sink or swim as befits their abilities?

The supervisor's response to Geoffrey's submission, sent into the department's transfer panel, strongly criticized its naïve and unconsidered adoption of a theoretical framework as well as various aspects of Geoffrey's writing. Two members of the department who had read the work concurred with the supervisor's reservations, and accordingly the panel adjourned transfer for six months, recommending that Geoffrey should do more work on his transfer report, take into account published critiques of Habermas, and resubmit it to a reconvened panel in the Spring.

Points for Consideration

- Is the student capable of refining his work sufficiently over the next 18 months to reach PhD standard?
- Has he been set unrealistic tasks?

Geoffrey's supervisory sessions with Professor Foster became increasingly difficult as he stubbornly refused to consider any criticisms of Habermas, or to recognize that he had applied the critic's methods too doggedly to the texts he was studying. His resubmitted piece in the Spring showed some signs of improvement in analytical thinking but was, if anything, even more informed by the paradigms of Habermas than before. Once again, Professor Foster was concerned about its style and told Geoffrey that, as it stood, his thesis would never make a book.

Shortly afterwards, Professor Foster had an arduous two hours supervisory meeting with Geoffrey that consisted of what was to all intents and purposes a critique of Geoffrey's writing. Going through Geoffrey's prose with him confirmed Professor Forster's conviction that research and writing were inextricably combined, and that the 'research' might derive from, or at least be refined by, Geoffrey's monitoring of the content and style of his own output. He pointed out to Geoffrey that writing of this kind was not just designed to 'communicate facts' – or to supply a running (and in this case doctrinaire) commentary upon the chosen text – but was heuristic or investigatory. It measured the assumptions and cultural imprints of the author's own critical discourse (and those of the critics to whom he was indebted) against those of the chosen body of texts. It was not a matter of 'writing up', but of drafting and then rewriting time and again until modalities of the critical and subject texts had found an appropriate or 'decorous' relationship with one another.

Points for Consideration

- Is the supervisor correct to decide that, even though he had mentioned Habermas, the outcome was unsatisfactory?
- Is the supervisor guilty of imposing his own criteria, as an effect of what Milton called 'answerable style' upon the student's prose?

Evolution of the problem

The student, without sufficient knowledge of classical languages might well be considered lacking the necessary background to undertake this research topic.

The supervisor did not follow up the student's references effectively. Lack of background knowledge plus a 'scraped' first-class degree should have precluded an offer being made.

Given the student had been accepted, the supervisor failed to provide enough support and guidance for the student in the early stages of his research. The one-year course the student undertook might not have been suitable.

The student lacked the required level of encouragement and enthusiastic support that a supervisor can provide. No attempt was made to build up a working and supportive relationship with the student, a relationship that can be mutually beneficial to both as the research progresses.

The supervision provided in this instance appeared to be an unsatisfactory 'top-down' arrangement, with no feeling that the supervisor was moving towards terms of academic equality with the student. Under such arrangements the supervisor may appear to the student to be imposing their own opinions and prejudices on the interpretations of the research, and this can sometimes, unwittingly or not, be correct. Perceptions by the student of such a heavy-handed approach, will not help the establishment of a fruitful working relationship between the student and the supervisor, and may also provoke unhelpful antagonism and rigid, unyielding responses from the student.

The student might have been allowed more time to rectify and improve the piece of work he wished to submit to the transfer panel.

The supervisor was undecided about the manner and style of writing that would best be followed by the student. Such indecision imparted to the student represents a lack of guidance and can only undermine student confidence in his writing.

There was insufficient contact and dialogue between the student and the supervisor which may contribute to the student's intransigence. The student can thus feel isolated, unsure of what is required and flounder unhappily in a mine of unworkable information.

The student was hampered in his progress due to lack of effective support and guidance, contact with his supervisor, and the demands by the supervisor, of unrealistic goals. Such goals can be unrealistic because of the student's lack of research capability. In addition, the student was being hindered by the supervisor due to the latter's heavy-handed insistence on the 'application' of theory. Dogmatic, unclarified and unexplained statements or demands can act as a constraint on a student's research development.

Possible prevention and resolution of the problem

1. Although the student gained a first-class degree, more scrutiny of his references, particularly through contact with the referees, and detailed appraisal of his background knowledge and qualifications could have established that he was unsuited to undertake the research project.
2. The student could have benefited from a greater level of support and guidance, particularly in regard to his shortcomings in classical languages. The availability of other appropriate courses, including Research Training Programme (RTP) modules could be explored.
3. The level and nature of the supervision could be improved, with increased meetings and dialogue and a less 'top-down', heavy-handed approach by the supervisor. Postponement of the student's transfer assessment coupled with a more sympathetic approach by the supervisor, might have allowed for a more positive decision by the transfer panel.
4. Current practice for most student–supervisor interactions is to build a working relationship between the individuals involved that will primarily benefit the student, and offer the greatest chance for students to realize their potential.
5. Both the supervisor's less than helpful management of the student and the less than optimal research abilities of the student contributed to this difficult situation. In this case, the advice and help of a co-supervisor, if one had been appointed from the outset, or the Graduate Tutor should have been sought. However, at this point it is up to the supervisor to recognize the problem and essentially encourage the student to apply hard work and the responsive attitude required to bring this PhD studentship to a positive outcome.
6. Should the student fail to meet the demands of the transfer panel, then he will be unable to progress towards his PhD.

8

An Issue of Scrutiny

Scenario

A circular sent to all departments by the International Recruitment Bureau (IRB) of the University of Camchester indicated that an arrangement had been reached with sections within the government of Thainam, an increasingly affluent country in Southeast Asia, to tap their rich resource of potential graduate students wishing to further their studies in the United Kingdom. The circular exhorted all departments at Camchester to find places for as many of these students as they possibly could, provided they met the university's academic and other criteria, as this could be of considerable benefit to the university in several ways.

Point for Consideration

- Can universities balance their global influences and requirements in attracting international graduate research students with their available resources in terms of manpower and facilities?

It just so happened that the Department of Mechanical Engineering at Camchester already had a single graduate student from Thainam, currently in his final year, whom the Head of Department had personally recruited from a previous overseas visit to Southeast Asia. The Head of Department also now had contacts among senior academic colleagues in Thainam and, following the university's request, asked them to recommend a potential PhD student to him. Soon after, Bhazot contacted the Head of Department explaining that he was the chosen student, who had been selected to study for a PhD at Camchester. The Head of Department then phoned Dr Mollberry, a lecturer colleague to tell him he had identified a new overseas student with funding to work with him on his research programme.

Points for Consideration

- What might the Head of Department have done before offering to accept a student on the basis of his previous experience?
- How best may potential graduate students from overseas be assessed for their suitability to a PhD research programme?

Bhazot turned out to be an unassuming individual, with an air of quiet confidence, and soon settled in. At his first meeting with Dr Mollberry to discuss the nature and direction of his research project, it soon became clear to Bhazot that his supervisor was somewhat vague about the proposed PhD programme and consequently, Bhazot began to wonder how much thought had gone into the preparation of it, and he informed Dr Mollberry of his concerns.

Point for Consideration

- How viable does a PhD project proposal have to be and who checks whether it is feasible or not?

Hastily, Dr Mollberry, with assistance from an academic colleague, managed to identify and outline, in broad terms, a somewhat modified research project which he thought Bhazot might find more appropriate and have more interest in. However, the 'cobbled together' research project only added to Bhazot's confusion as to what he was supposed to be doing, but as time was moving on, and Bhazot was keen to get started, the project went ahead.

Dr Mollberry's initial directive to his new student required him to write a report encompassing a literature search of what appeared to be a fairly general topic, and to couple this with a written exposition, that would highlight one or more specific problems within the research area that might be targeted, and also to indicate what possible avenues or strategies might be used to approach and resolve the problems he identified.

Dr Mollberry duly received Bhazot's report, which although it was a brave effort to get to grips with the research area, gave little indication that the student had any understanding of the nature of research work as an intellectual exercise of exploration, involving the development and testing of hypotheses using rigorously applied, and stringently controlled methods. Unfortunately for Dr Mollberry, Bhazot had also been unable to identify a single route forward that could be used to direct the research, and which might profitably be pursued to resolve the problem.

The area of Bhazot's proposed research was, as Dr Mollberry was well aware, vague and confusing and despite Bhazot's determination to relate to the research project, he was unable to make any real progress.

Points for Consideration

- Is the supervisor facing up to reality in this situation?
- What action might the student be advised to take at this stage?

A few months later, Bhazot's project was still not going anywhere and although he was starting to get concerned about his future, whenever he met the Head of Department or Dr Mollberry, Bhazot was always reassured that things would look up in the future. About six months after Bhazot had commenced his research programme the situation became much more serious when Bhazot met his personal tutor, Professor Jones, for the first time to discuss, among other things, Bhazot's progress and the feasibility of the project. It soon became clear to Professor Jones that the project as outlined by Dr Mollberry was a 'half-baked' idea that just wouldn't stand up to detailed scrutiny. In Professor Jones's opinion, the only solution was to get the project changed as soon as possible.

Point for Consideration

- Under what circumstances can a research project be significantly changed?

Not surprisingly, Bhazot was very upset at the outcome of his meeting with Professor Jones, although somewhat relieved at the thought of a possible resolution to his current predicament. Fortunately for Bhazot, Professor Jones was very keen to find him a project that would go somewhere. Professor Jones decided the best course of action would be to discuss this matter directly with the Head of Department without involving Dr Mollberry, as Professor Jones had lost confidence in the latter's supervisory abilities.

Points for Consideration

- Who is responsible for the time the student wasted on the first project?
- Is there any way the student can be compensated for wasted time and money?

Following the meeting of Professor Jones with the Head of Department, a new project was proposed for Bhazot which involved studies of some relevance to Thainam under the supervision of Dr Khang, who was particularly interested in studying research topics relevant to Southeast Asia. Dr Khang was a wise choice as he always put forward detailed research proposals to students and consulted them widely before finally agreeing on the definitive study. On reflection, the Head of Department realized that Dr Mollberry's approach to proposing a research project to Bhazot was far from ideal and came to the conclusion that the current system for setting up research projects must be improved, through discussions with the Graduate Tutor.

Points for Consideration

- Who influences policy-making for improving graduate student affairs?
- Can a department make decisions unilaterally about how best to manage graduate student activities?

So now seven months into his research programme, Bhazot began a new project with Dr Khang. Once he had good direction, Bhazot turned out to be an excellent student and although he completed his PhD in just over three years, his registration period was a disappointing four years and was a poor reflection of his work-rate under the well-organized Dr Khang.

Evolution of the problem

The selection and admission of the student were poorly managed. There seemed to be no communication between the supervisor and student concerning the nature of the project. The prime reason for admission was based on the availability of a qualified student who had funding.

The student and/or student's sponsor should have been more pro-active about the nature of research project that was required.

The student was accepted for an MPhil/PhD, at least partially on the basis of university, rather than departmental, supervisor or research requirements; the Head of Department was under some pressure to make the appointment.

The initial supervisor seemed to have been chosen at random to take on the student and appeared to be totally unprepared. Even when the student arrived in the department, the proposed research programme appeared vague and ill-defined.

In the early stages of the initial research programme, the student clearly had doubts about the project himself but found it difficult to complain as the Head of Department was partly involved with overseeing the student's activities.

Ideally, the personal tutor or even the Graduate Tutor should have been consulted by the student at an earlier stage.

Possible prevention and resolution of the problem

1. It is unacceptable for a student to be admitted onto an ill-conceived research programme. Formal peer-review of research grants and studentships allows for the quality of projects to be monitored. More recently,

some departments have developed in-house peer-review of projects to maintain the quality of the proposals.

2. The student might well not have been accepted under normal circumstances, but there was subtle pressure from the university to accept students from this particular country if at all possible. Selection of graduate research students should be based on perceived student ability and the availability of supervisors in the relevant area of research, not the student's nationality.

3. A fairly early formal meeting of the student with his personal tutor highlighted the difficulties the student was experiencing with the initial project. However, apart from issues surrounding peer-review mentioned above, it would have been better if the student had complained to the personal tutor or Graduate Tutor at an earlier stage.

4. A change of research project is probably acceptable until the end of year one or at the transfer stage. Presumably, an inappropriate project will always be detected at transfer and it is inconceivable to think that this problem could occur in the second year or later. If the latter were true, this would significantly affect submission of the thesis.

5. It is the university's responsibility to compensate the student, both in time period for submission of the thesis and in cost, if an ill-conceived or inappropriate project was proposed for the student to undertake.

9

An Issue of Transfer

Scenario

Dr Gillian Butterworth's research output had been on the decline of late and, under pressure from the Head of Department, she had agreed to accept Adam for a university studentship concerned with the influence of art on Spanish literature in the seventeenth century. Disappointingly, Adam was the only applicant, and he had just about scraped a 2:1 degree from Camford University.

Points for Consideration

- Should supervisors be pressurized into taking on research students, especially if the student may not be the most promising?
- Is a 2:1 degree the most appropriate basic level for entry onto a research degree programme?

In the first semester, Dr Butterworth allowed Adam to settle in, and met with him only once or twice over this period, using the meetings to explain, in detail, how he should approach his topic in the first year. By the second semester, Dr Butterworth arranged to see Adam for more formal meetings to discuss his research progress whenever Adam thought he needed them. However, the arrangement was not particularly successful as several months passed without any contact between them. It was only towards the end of the second semester, when the date of Adam's transfer meeting had been set, that he requested a meeting with his supervisor. At the meeting, Dr Butterworth was disappointed with both the volume and quality of Adam's research work, and on reflection after the meeting became increasingly concerned about his impending transfer meeting.

Points for Consideration

- How might perceptions held by the student, and sometimes by the supervisor, that there is little necessity for urgency in year one of a PhD research programme, be overcome?
- How might the importance of time management in research planning be stressed in the first year?
- Why might the supervisor have shown little concern with the progress of the student in the first year?

At the transfer meeting, it was clear Adam had done some acceptable work for his literature review. However, the assessment panel felt he had made insufficient progress with his research and had a poor knowledge and understanding of the concepts on which his work was based. The progress report from Dr Butterworth confirmed the views of the panel, and they were confident that a failed transfer was the correct decision. The panel advised Adam where his deficiencies lay and reminded him he had one further chance to transfer onto the PhD track; otherwise he would remain an MPhil student. Adam was disappointed at the outcome and sought a meeting with his supervisor to try and fix the problem in time for his final transfer attempt, set for five months ahead. The meeting proved constructive, as both Adam and Dr Butterworth seemed concerned about the transfer setback. It was decided supervisory meetings every three to four weeks would be required, and accordingly, a series of dates for these were set.

Points for Consideration

- Where does the fault for this failure primarily lie?
- Who makes the final decision and shoulders the responsibility for the transfer?
- What should be the role of the transfer panel in the transfer process?

Adam turned up to discuss his research progress with Dr Butterworth on only the first two of the set occasions, although she was ready for his visits at most of the other agreed times. However, at the meeting pre-arranged for a date just prior to his final assessment by the transfer panel, Adam appeared promptly and, it seemed to Dr Butterworth, confident that his research was sufficiently on track to warrant successful transfer. However, as the meeting wore on, Dr Butterworth again became concerned about Adam's progress and his grasp of the topic, and felt both disappointed and let down, although in spite of his failure to appear at earlier meetings, Adam seemed very committed to a future career in research.

> **Points for Consideration**
>
> - Whose responsibility is it to arrange supervisory meetings?
> - Has the supervisor been negligent in not 'chasing up' the student, given the importance of the second transfer meeting?
> - Are the behaviour and attitude of the student in this situation appropriate and acceptable?
> - Could the poor showing of the student at the transfer meeting have been improved through prior actions by the supervisor?

At his final transfer meeting, Adam was far from convincing and the panel, having received a less than positive and somewhat ambiguous progress report from Dr Butterworth, were disappointed with both the student's performance and research progress, and reluctantly felt they had no choice but to recommend he continue his studies for an MPhil.

When Adam was informed of the panel's decision, he was extremely angry, his anger being largely directed at Dr Butterworth. He blamed lack of guidance and insufficient commitment by his supervisor as the prime reasons for his failure. Dr Butterworth was upset at the allegations and reminded Adam of the agreed meeting schedule which he had failed to fulfil. Adam claimed Dr Butterworth was rarely available and had been unhelpful even when he was able to meet with her. He demanded a further transfer attempt. A week later, Dr Butterworth was shocked to hear Adam had appealed against the transfer decision, claiming irresponsible and negligent supervision. Dr Butterworth believed the panel's decision had been correct, and certainly felt that, given all the circumstances, her supervision had not contributed to Adam's transfer failure.

> **Points for Consideration**
>
> - Has the student any justification for taking his situation to appeal?
> - Is the supervisor right to feel aggrieved over the student's action?
> - How might the supervisor defend her position against the appeal?

Evolution of the problem

In the euphoria of starting a research programme many students may regard the transfer procedure as a mere formality. Research students will normally be unable to gauge either the extent or the quality of their research progress over the first two years of the degree.

So many graduates are now awarded a 2:1 degree that it is debatable whether this is sufficient to be considered as automatic entry to a higher research degree. In the selection of top-class students for research degrees, arguably only those awarded a first-class degree should be considered. Only one applicant and the quality of the student's degree, 'just scraping a 2:1', are not ideal for admission to a research degree.

Both the motivation and the capabilities of the supervisor were questionable. The track record of the supervisor's research might be less than adequate, and the Head of Department's action in pressuring her to accept a relatively poor quality student, was unwise.

The student was not given sufficient information about the nature of the research degree. At the commencement of a research degree programme, most students will have little idea of what is required and the pace at which it will be necessary to work.

There is a need to attempt early progress with the research work in the first semester of a research degree, as time, as at all stages of the research programme, is at a premium. This is especially so at the outset of the studies as a number of hurdles will have to be cleared in the first year.

The supervisor could have been more forceful in convincing the student of the need for more meetings.

The student failed to heed the advice of the assessment panel and to take full advantage of the help offered by his supervisor.

Possible prevention and resolution of the problem

1. A discussion between all parties in the department involved in the appointment and allocation of research students might have prevented either the appointment of this student to a research degree, or his allocation to this particular supervisor.
2. The student might not have the ability to complete a research degree and take up a research career, but might not have realized his limitations. Earlier assessment of the situation, accompanied by different decisions, could have avoided the wasted year.
3. Regular meetings can enable the supervisor to judge the extent and quality of the student's research progress, and indicate this to the student, along with advice as to both short-term and long-term goals and the requirements to remain on track. The supervisor should not have left it to the student to assess his own progress.
4. Because of long-term considerations, the student should have been encouraged to commence his research work as soon as possible, and certainly as soon as the supervisor was satisfied his background knowledge and understanding of the work were adequate.
5. The transfer panel provides independent advice on whether to recommend student transfer from MPhil to PhD. Usually, however, the actual responsibility for recommending the upgrade remains with the

supervisor, although the support of the transfer panel may be of considerable use to the supervisor.

6. At some point between the two transfer meetings, the supervisor, the student and the departmental Graduate Tutor and/or the Head of Department should have met with the student to discuss the situation and provide advice about the way forward.

7. Although it was on the panel's advice that the student was not transferred to a PhD programme, it is the supervisor who stands accused of negligence and irresponsibility towards the student. A supervisor should ensure that appropriate documentation with regard to student–supervisor meetings and progress records is available. A meeting log of all formal meetings with the student should be maintained, and include signatures on completed, agreed, forms confirming the student was aware of details of his research progress at all times.

8. The basis for a resolution will be made at the appeal hearing. Although the supervisor may have been slack in organizing meetings and record keeping, an independent panel was instrumental in deciding the student's fate at two transfer meetings. It is unlikely that the student's appeal would be upheld, and that he would be given a further chance at transfer.

9. Student appeals are probably becoming more common. By bringing an appeal, the student will damage his relationship with the supervisor. The second or co-supervisor will play an important role in helping the student to prepare for completion of the MPhil. If a replacement supervisor is not possible, then joint supervision for completion of the MPhil would be the most appropriate action.

10. The reason for the transfer failure should be explained to the student, and he should, of course, be given every encouragement to work hard towards successful completion of an MPhil degree. It could be suggested to him that an apology to his supervisor would be helpful.

10

An Issue of Progress

Scenario

It was a hot June, and Alistair, in the second year of his PhD, was looking forward to a long summer break backpacking around Portugal with friends he'd met at the University of Wardchester. He'd enjoyed his first year planning his research programme with his supervisor and getting it up and running. His end-of-year review of his research and his transfer onto his PhD programme had proceeded smoothly, and as his second year had commenced, Alistair had gained the distinct impression that he was regarded by both the department, and by his supervisor, as a student with a promising research future.

Points for Consideration

- What is the major role of the supervisor in the first year of an MPhil/PhD programme?
- Should motivation of a student be necessary in their first year, and if so, how is this achieved?

Since then, however, things had been somewhat flat to Alistair. His research work, concerned with the erosion of local suburban facilities and amenities arising through the development and construction of post-millennium sub-domes, now seemed to him to be proving something of a damp squib. His methodology, based on questionnaires and their analysis, pressure group interviews and projection modelling techniques, seemed to lack momentum, to be boring and uninteresting, and for him, at least, had failed to crystallize into a coherent and strategically relevant picture.

Points for Consideration

- Why does this student appear to have lost research momentum and enthusiasm in his second year?
- How may student expectations of their studies be met at this stage of their work?
- How may the strategic relevance of a student's research be conveyed to the student?
- Who is responsible for maintaining student motivation in the second year?

Anyhow, the stimulating pressures and excitement of the first year, were now in the past for Alistair, his summer holidays were about to commence, while write-up, thesis submission and examination were still a long way off, or so it seemed to him. Alistair felt confident about his abilities, and felt that the year or so ahead would be very straightforward and easy now that the work for the coming months was planned, his research survey was underway and he had completed a few of his interviews. He had also located some exciting night-life spots in Wardchester, and he could look forward to a great social life in the coming, dreary and cold northern winter. He had also taken up rugby football again, a sport he had dropped during the first year of his PhD to make time for his research. The rugby training and the matches should provide some compensation for his waning interest in his research project, which, to all intents and purposes, seemed to him to have become a simple 'handle-turning' exercise. With his summer holidays in the offing, it looked to Alistair that the near future would be most enjoyable and undemanding.

Points for Consideration

- Should it be necessary to guard against over-confidence in a research student?
- Should it be necessary for a supervisor to maintain motivation and focus in a student during the second year of a PhD research programme?
- How may student complacency with regard to their research work be overcome?

Alistair had been meeting his supervisor every six weeks or so since the start of his first year, but latterly, the meetings had been short as Alistair had not much to report. His major survey was up and running, but could not be statistically evaluated, analysed and interpreted for at least another few months. Interviews with one of the pressure groups were complete, but a further five groups had yet to be seen. In his mind, Alistair had decided to deal with the rest of the interviews in the coming autumn, and at the same time start to tackle the projection modelling work. At their last, somewhat longer, research meeting, his supervisor, although seeming somewhat preoccupied with administrative and undergraduate examination matters, had commented that Alistair's research programme seemed to be progressing well, looked problem-free with clear goals and a clear way forward for the coming year, and all this had confirmed Alistair's personal assessment of his situation. He and his supervisor had then spent a further hour or so planning Alistair's work for the next few months in some detail, after which his supervisor had told him to make sure he had a good holiday break to recover from all his excellent and hard work over the first year.

Points for Consideration

- Do you consider that the frequency and form of the student–supervisor meetings are adequate for this student?
- Is the supervisor encouraging, albeit implicitly, the research independence of this student at too early a stage in his research development?

Two or three weeks later as he looked back on this meeting, Alistair remained very content about his prospects in his second year research programme. He was, however, vaguely aware that the few questionnaires so far returned in his major survey that he had found time to glance at, seemed open to some misinterpretation and ambiguities, and gave the impression of being less helpful than he had anticipated. Should he have brought this to the attention of his supervisor? On balance, he thought, probably not. He still had plenty of time, most of the questionnaires were still to come in, his supervisor had been very busy, and in planning his work for his second year, his supervisor had alluded to the questionnaire several times, without indicating that it would be anything other than straightforward. Also, his own instincts, which had not let him down as yet, told him not to worry, everything would be OK, and his summer holiday was imminent – here comes summer and an easy life!

Points for Consideration

- Is the student's acceptance of his second-year research situation a realistic one?
- Is the supervisor giving the right impressions and offering good advice to the student?

Evolution of the problem

Both student and supervisor appear too complacent about the future progress of the research work. Only in very exceptional circumstances might a PhD be straightforward and provide 'an easy ride'.

Due to an excellent first year, a naturally confident and good student has become over-confident, and this has been reinforced by the supervisor.

The research programme may not be challenging or stimulating enough for the student, and this, coupled with the rapid and straightforward progress the student made in his first year, might be promoting a loss of motivation and interest in the research project.

It must be recognized that even good students will be inexperienced in planning a research programme, and will be unaware of the appropriate timescales required to complete their work, and the pitfalls and problems that often arise during a research programme.

The supervisor has failed to alert the student to the possibility of unforeseen difficulties that can sometimes occur during the course of a research programme, and has also, perhaps unintentionally, created or reinforced, the student's own impression that there are no severe time constraints on the research work.

The student has failed to alert the supervisor to a possible problem with one aspect of the research programme that could cause future difficulties.

Possible prevention and resolution of the problem

1. The student should be informed at the outset of his research work that there are likely to be difficult periods when the research work may be progressing slowly, and that it may be necessary to modify timescales according to how the work moves along.
2. The student needs to be well aware of the timescales associated with his research programme, and where research methodology may be cumbersome and time-consuming.
3. Motivation of the student through the second year should be maintained through, for example, regular and frequent and informal contact with the supervisor; delivery, by the student, of any completed work through departmental seminars or at appropriate conferences; organizing some of the data already gathered into the form suitable for publication or for inclusion in the thesis.
4. It is to be hoped that by the end of the first year, the working relationship between the student and supervisor will be sufficiently established that the student can inform the supervisor of any reservations, however minor, he may have about his research studies. Conversely, the supervisor must always provide the student with the opportunity to air any research-related, or other problems he may have that might impinge on the progress of his work.

11

An Issue of Judgement

Scenario

Ali, a 35-year-old graduate student with a Master's degree in Applied Mathematics from the State University of Upama, a small, oil-rich country in the Middle East, had arrived with his wife and three children in the United Kingdom one year ago to embark on a PhD degree in the Department of Statistical Probability at the University of Westhampton. On his arrival, Ali had successfully completed an English language course, and had immediately entered into discussions regarding his PhD programme with Dr Willis Young, a lecturer in statistics, one year into his first academic post.

Points for Consideration

- Is it appropriate to allocate a mature student, with a family, and from a different cultural background, to a young and inexperienced supervisor?
- What support could have been provided to the supervisor?

Dr Young had agreed to 'take on' Ali, as his first ever PhD student after discussions with his Head of Department, who had informed Dr Young that, although he realized this was not the ideal situation, all other staff in the dpartment were already overburdened with graduate students, and the university 'required' the department to take as many overseas students as possible. He informed Dr Young that Ali had been marked out as a potentially good prospect by the university's representative on his most recent visit to Upama several months earlier. Ali was funded by his country's government who were keen to build up a body of well-qualified statisticians to boost, expand and export their country's newly-designed health economics programme. Dr Young's research programme would receive substantial financial support if he agreed to supervise Ali. In the face of all this Dr Young accepted Ali as his research student, reasoning that as a most promising, yet mature student, with a good command of English, supervision should be plain sailing.

Points for Consideration

- Does the Head of Department have any other options for dealing with this student?
- What might be the supervisor's best course of action in this situation?

Although all went well over the first year, and Ali felt reasonably satisfied with his progress during this period, he was mindful of the senior and demanding governmental post that awaited him and that he was expected to fill immediately on his return to his home country. He was thus a little concerned that a number of statistical programme applications and systems that he felt would be valuable assets for him to learn and acquire an up-to-date working knowledge of, had not yet been included in his research studies. He had been at pains to mention these to his supervisor at their initial discussions and had gained the impression, at the time, that Dr Young had perceived the importance to Ali of incorporating these advanced statistical packages and systems into the research programme he had outlined to Ali, in some detail. Ali had raised this matter again in subsequent research meetings with his supervisor during the first year, but so far he had not been asked to apply them to his studies.

Point for Consideration

- To what extent, if any, should a research supervisor accommodate any specific needs of a student in designing a PhD research programme, for example, via some form of training needs analysis?

As the second year progressed, Ali became even more uneasy as, in the regular monthly meetings with Dr Young, it seemed to him that his programme of research as set out at the start of the first year, was not following the direction he wished, and he was unable to perceive how the methodologies he needed to learn could be woven into his current research activities. However, he thought, he had been at pains to make Dr Young well aware of the importance of his stipulations, and his supervisor would surely be able to find a way of meeting Ali's needs. However, Dr Young surprised and dismayed Ali by unexpectedly announcing a change of direction for Ali's research work involving an approach using a group of systems analyses that he wished Ali to try, applications that were completely new to Ali. Furthermore, the statistical programme application packages which Ali desperately needed to have experience of, would apparently play no part in this new line of research. During a series of meetings with his supervisor to discuss this turn of events, Ali in attempting to follow the career agenda he considered both important and necessary for himself and for his country, sought, increasingly forcefully, to again explain his requirements to Dr Young and make his supervisor understand his concerns. The response he constantly received was that the work that Ali must follow represented a logical and exciting progression stemming from an element of their work over the first year, and would surely provide strong support if Ali could pull it off, for an extremely interesting and novel finding, which might well provide Ali with at least two publications and could be the 'making' of his PhD thesis.

Points for Consideration

- Who is at fault in the degeneration of this working relationship?
- Could the different cultural backgrounds of the student and supervisor be playing a role in this situation?
- Are the student's requirements unreasonable?
- Whose judgement would it be advisable to follow in these circumstances?

Almost in desperation at their next meeting, Ali referred Dr Young back to his original research programme outline and informed him with some asperity, that there was a written record from their earlier meetings which showed they had agreed Ali would use certain, specific statistical programme applications and systems in which he particularly wished to become adept. Dr Young's response to his student's outburst was that Ali had lost all understanding of the overall aims of his research programme, and indeed, what a PhD was all about, and would have difficulty gaining his PhD if there was no obviously novel aspect to his work. This, he added, could only be achieved if Ali followed Dr Young's research guidance and instructions. Dr Young also said he himself had little experience of the particular statistical applications Ali wished to use, they were outside his field, and anyway Ali's research had progressed well beyond the stage at which these methods could be applied.

Point for Consideration

- Might a compromise still be possible from these entrenched, yet not unreasonable positions?

Immediately following this meeting Ali went to the Head of Department with a request to be transferred from Dr Young's supervision because he felt that both he and his programme of work were not being adequately supervised.

Points for Consideration

- Is the final course of action adopted by the student a wise one?
- Has the supervisor handled his working relationship with the student with an appropriate level of tact and expediency over the course of the PhD programme to date?
- What courses of action are open to the Head of Department?

Evolution of the problem

Due to inexperience, the supervisor expected the student to follow his research strategy without question, and made no allowance for any abilities the student might have to think for himself. The supervisor also failed to realize the importance to the student of his subsequent career in his home country, and the specific, yet relevant, research skills he needed to acquire through his PhD programme.

The difference in the background culture, levels of experience and maturity between the student and the supervisor made communication and the establishment of a clear working relationship between them less than straightforward.

A young, inexperienced supervisor placed in this position may act in a somewhat headstrong way, and wish to establish his authority over a student who may be perceived, because of his background, as being less able as a researcher, even though that student is somewhat older than the supervisor. As a consequence, the supervisor may feel the need to prove his supervisory capabilities and override or fail to consider reasonable student requirements.

The allocation of this particular student to this particular inexperienced supervisor was a management error by the Head of Department.

The supervisor should not have allowed the situation to reach crisis point and should have addressed the problem at the outset of the research programme.

The judgement of the student was clouded by the burden of his requirements for his future career, which overrode his understanding of the importance and value of a good PhD. He was also, in all probability, placing too much weight on the perceived demands of his funding body and his future career.

The problem presents some difficulty, as both student and supervisor, arguably, have justifiable positions.

Possible prevention and resolution of the problem

1. From the student's background, it may be assumed that he wishes to pursue his PhD at that particular institution and in that particular

department, as the expertise and the technology he particularly wants to acquire are well established there. If so, the supervisor should have been aware of the methodologies, and even if not proficient in them himself, by taking advice and help from departmental colleagues, should have found it possible to incorporate them into the student's research programme. The appointment of a co-supervisor would have been invaluable in helping to resolve this problem.

2. Although it is normally inadvisable to allocate a mature student to an inexperienced supervisor, in the circumstances, there was little alternative for the Head of Department. It would have been advisable, however, for an experienced co-supervisor to have been appointed to help resolve the initial 'misunderstandings' as the research programme was being established.

3. If he had taken it on board, the supervisor should have brought the student's request for specific methodologies to be used in his research to the attention of the Graduate Tutor, a more experienced colleague or the Head of Department.

4. The supervisor, due either to his failure to recognize or to his intransigence over the student's request to use certain methodologies, was primarily to blame for the student's increasing concerns as the first year progressed. His working relationship with the student should have been conducted with greater tact and consideration. The student was also partly at fault in not bringing his needs to the attention of the Graduate Tutor at an early stage, although his different cultural background could have prevented him from doing so.

5. At this point in the research programme, there is still time to accede to the student's requirements. This can be done through immediate action by the Head of Department, but must include consideration of the views of the supervisor, and particularly the supervisor's overview of the final form of the research thesis submission.

6. In view of the very promising nature of the PhD research work, however, changing the supervisor as requested by the student is probably inadvisable, due to time constraints, the amount of work already completed and the, to-date, successful outcomes of that work. It might be possible to persuade the student to pursue the research lines as laid out by the supervisor, and if necessary, in support of this, the Head of Department or the Graduate Tutor might wish, in consultation with the student, to contact the representatives of the student's sponsors in the United Kingdom.

7. Both student and supervisor should be appraised as to the nature of the PhD, with respect to the expectations of both, and the nature of the boundaries of each individual's responsibilities.

12

An Issue of Distance

Jerry Wellington

Scenario

Jimmy Cassar lives on the Mediterranean island of Menta, working for a government department dealing with Education and Skills. He had successfully completed his first degree 27 years earlier; later, while in full-time employment, he successfully completed a Master's degree at one of the Russell group universities in the UK. This gave him the thirst and motivation to go further. At the mature age of 47, Jimmy decided to enrol for a professional doctorate at the University of Shepperley. He chose Shepperley because it runs a professional doctorate course for those who already have Master's degrees, and he chose the department at Shepperley because it had received high ratings for both teaching and research in the last round of assessment exercises and this was clearly shown on the website. When exploring the site, Jimmy also studied the interests, publications, expertise and experience of the staff involved. He was able to identify two members of staff who, although he had never met them, looked like ideal supervisors for his field of interest. He chose a professional doctorate because it offered a structured programme: phase one provided a series of modules that introduced students to research methods and methodology; phase two was the thesis stage, in which the student would be closely supervised in completing a piece of original research related to their own professional interest and practice.

Points for Consideration

- What might motivate a mature individual to become a 'distance learner', rather than to study at home?
- What is the motivation behind a student selecting a professional doctorate, as opposed to the more 'traditional' PhD?
- Could the student have done anything more towards the organization of his arrangements for meeting the demands of his course, and selecting his supervisor?

Although originally an English teacher, Jimmy's work as an adviser and policy-maker in the government department on Menta involved him in giving advice and creating policy statements for teachers in Menta's secondary schools. He was given particular responsibility by the Menta Government for implementing their recent push which was 'driving' new technology (Information Communication Technology, as they termed it) into Menta's schools, sometimes against the teachers' will or better judgement. This was exactly the area he wished to explore in his thesis. Accordingly, Jimmy applied to, and was accepted for the doctorate course at the University of Shepperley.

The UK option certainly looked attractive for Jimmy as long as the face-to-face teaching that was involved occurred only twice a year, and there were plenty of cheap flights. The first two weekends of the initial phase of the course were in winter, which provided the advantage of off-peak slots, and the cut-price airlines could get him to Manchester and back for the price of the train fare across the Pennines. He had a slight shock concerning the summer weekend, when the air fares doubled, but he felt he would be able to cope.

All went well over the first, modular, phase of his doctorate, and he duly entered the second research thesis stage, of the structured programme.

Points for Consideration

- Did the student think ahead far enough concerning the final stages of the course, and the communication problems that might be involved?
- What other factors might a mature, part-time student be expected to take into account before embarking on a commitment to a professional doctorate programme?

During this thesis phase, he arranged regular face-to-face meetings with his supervisor, Dr Shotts, trying to average about three such meetings per year. These were arranged around Jimmy's business trips to the UK, visits to his relations in London and his occasional holiday in Northern Europe. At first, Dr Shotts suggested dates for meetings that suited his own timetable and other commitments, but soon realized that he would need to be more flexible and accommodating to fit in with Jimmy's time and money management.

Jimmy was promoted twice in his government department during his doctorate, perhaps as an effect of his engagement in it, but he was not quite sure. Promotion is one of the hazards for any part-time, mature student in a full-time job, and the effects on part-time commitments can be exacerbated by distance, especially if frequent face-to-face meetings are needed and the department insists upon such commitments. Travel takes time, and the commitments have to be juggled when organizing and planning any trips. This is especially true for someone with family commitments. Jimmy had two teenage daughters and an adult son who had just purchased a house.

Point for Consideration

- To what extent and in what way, will time management skills be of importance to a distance learner?

Although Dr Shotts was well read and keen to work with Jimmy, he knew almost nothing about working in Menta and the difficulties facing the Menta government's drive to push ICT into education. Dr Shotts had only visited Menta once and had been unable to visit many schools at the time; even then, he was treated like a visitor from overseas (which he was) and gained little insight into the real situation in the island's secondary schools. However, he very conscientiously made the effort to read widely and tried to impress his student with references from the student's own context. Unfortunately, he found little or nothing in the refereed journals on Menta and ICT. Dr Shotts remained truly 'Anglo-centric', even although he hated to admit it.

Writing is a painful process for most people, and some have even likened it to giving birth or having a tooth removed. These are probably not helpful analogies but the process of getting a long thesis, in Jimmy's case around 50,000 words, onto paper is a difficult and very time-consuming one, especially for Jimmy as his local language of conversation was not English. Jimmy's written work needed regular and frequent correction and scrutinizing by Dr Shotts. Jimmy wanted feedback from his supervisor on one section of his thesis at a time, and he sent his work in, in draft form, a chunk at a time. Huge e-mail attachments posed a problem for Dr Shotts (who had eight other students to supervise) so when a whole chapter was ready it was posted. This took about six days to arrive, and it was essential that the supervisor did not 'sit on it' for a long period before providing Jimmy with feedback.

For most purposes electronic contact worked well between Jimmy and Dr Shotts. Jimmy did not have to wait for more than a few days for a response, unless Dr Shotts was away from his department, and this was always agreed and notified in advance, by both parties. Although it lacked some of the richness of the face-to-face meetings, the cups of tea, the chit-chat, the body language and the jokes, the partnership worked well. E-mail was used for quick questions (of the 'Am I on the right lines?' variety), for conveying information about progress, and for sending drafts of chapters (though Dr Shotts did ask for hard copy when large chunks of writing were involved). The e-mails also provided a means for Dr Shotts to offer encouragement, praise and support to Jimmy, a hugely important affective domain in learning, which is as vital to mature 47-year-olds as it is to school students.

Points for Consideration

- What factors are of major importance for the supervisor to take into consideration in accepting and progressing a student undertaking a higher degree through 'distance' learning?
- What else might the supervisor do to ensure his suitability to manage a student undertaking a higher degree as a 'distance' learner?
- Can e-mail ever be as effective as face-to-face contact in maintaining the affective domain of the supervisory process?

However, although the doctoral programme at the University of Shepperley had set up a facility for students to converse with each other via Web CT (Course Tools) (a virtual learning environment (VLE), similar to First Class and Blackboard) due to his work and family commitments, Jimmy really did not have time to log on to it during his thesis writing. He could not really justify the time spent logging onto and contributing to a VLE. He did make attempts to keep in touch with others in the cohort socially by phone and e-mail, but there was also something unsatisfactory, almost unreal, about this, and Jimmy also felt much the same about the affective side of supervision (praise, support, chivvying, motivating) which always seemed to be more effective face-to-face. This lack of effective and telling communication between Jimmy, his supervisor and his peers on the professional doctorate programme, and the troubles and time involved in dispatching his written material and dealing with Dr Shotts, affected Jimmy considerably at this difficult, write-up stage. It all seemed so remote and unreal compared to his family life, his career and his work on Menta. Jimmy's enthusiasm and motivation to complete the final stages of his doctorate were seriously eroded.

Although Jimmy was apparently trying his best at thesis writing, Dr Shotts wondered if there was anything else that could be done to help him. The last thing he wanted now was for Jimmy to give up at the final hurdle.

Points for Consideration

- What incentives can be provided to keep students, especially 'distance' learners, engaged with a virtual learning environment such as Web CT?
- Might a mature student holding an important, full-time job request some time off from his work at the time of his thesis write-up?
- What factors might govern his employer's decision on this? To what extent should the supervisor consider the family commitments of the student in demanding full-time devotion to the work at the write-up stage?

Evolution of the problem

A student's decision to become a 'distance' learner, rather than study in their home country, or choose to take up a professional doctorate instead of the 'traditional' PhD programme will be influenced by many factors. The decision may sometimes be taken without sufficient consideration of what is entailed, or for the wrong reasons. Such unconsidered or unwise decisions almost always lead to difficulties and problems at some point during the attempt to acquire the qualification.

Although the initial phase of the professional doctorate, because of its defined and structured nature, was manageable for the student in terms of time and costs, the increased contact that was most appropriate for the thesis phase meant that this was less structured, less manageable, and consequently created greater demands on time and finances for the student. There are likely to be many pressures for a 'mature' student, especially for one in a demanding job and/or with a family and dependent or partially-dependent children.

It is sometimes extremely difficult for a supervisor to have the necessary expertise in a given student's research project area. Supervisors may misjudge or overestimate their competence and understanding of a particular research area, and may unwisely accept a student on a less than secure background knowledge.

The student felt increasingly isolated from his peers, and from the research ambience of the department in the thesis phase of his doctorate, and these factors, together with the difficult and cumbersome nature of his contact with the supervisor in progressing his thesis write-up, plus the prolonged process of the part-time doctorate, led to an increasing loss of the student's enthusiasm and motivation. For a variety of reasons, including time, it can be difficult for the supervisor to acquire the necessary detailed and working knowledge of the student's line of research as the project progresses, especially when the student's background and thesis topic are set at a distance, and in a foreign country.

Electronic mail can certainly help to maintain close contact between student and supervisor – but it does not have the richness of nuance of face-to-face contact. Far more information, advice and understanding can be transmitted through 'face-to-face' contact in meetings. Virtual Learning Environments, such as Web CT can help to organize and deliver a course, but the students involved with this need incentives to log on and engage with the process.

Motivation can often become an important issue if the supervisor is not able, for whatever reason, to give feedback on submitted work in good time. This can be further exacerbated if English is not the student's first language, and necessitates a greater amount of scrutiny, assessment and correction by the supervisor.

Possible prevention and resolution of the problem

1. A mature individual holding first and Master's degrees should ensure that their reasons for undertaking a 'distance' doctorate, as opposed to studying in their own country, are valid and very carefully thought through.
2. The student's decision to undertake a professional doctorate was correct as there is increasing convergence between the newer routes to a PhD, involving research training and a structured build-up, and the professional doctorates.
3. The student may possibly have found a more suitable supervisor by further internet searching, in particular, a supervisor with greater knowledge of the local situations pertaining to his proposed area of research, and a supervisor who was somewhat less 'Anglo-centric'.
4. In accepting and managing overseas students, supervisors need to be aware of, and reflect on, their 'Anglo-centricity', even if they cannot completely overcome it.
5. The supervisor must also be aware of any shortcomings he may feel he has both in his suitability to manage a mature, part-time learner from overseas and in his knowledge and understanding of the subject matter the student wishes to research. The supervisor should seek advice and help in the management of this type of student, if he feels it appropriate, from the Head of Department, Graduate Tutor or more experienced colleagues who may be available, and, most importantly, transmit such information and views to the prospective student at the outset, so the latter can make an informed decision on accepting the offer and/or the supervisor. Presumably there is an optimum number of students that a supervisor can be responsible for and this supervisor with a total of nine students must have been under considerable pressure.
6. The long duration of a part-time doctoral degree means that a student embarking on such a programme, must consider all factors, such as finance, work and family commitments, that may play a significant part in the management of this course of action. When this study is undertaken by the individual as a 'distance' learner, this must, clearly, also be taken into account.
7. Other unforeseen factors, such as change of circumstances in work, or unexpected family events should also be considered by any mature student undertaking a part-time programme of study leading to a doctorate.
8. Distance learners are normally highly motivated, but this needs to be sustained and nurtured. Encouragement and support must be provided alongside intellectual guidance and supervision; the affective is as important as the cognitive domain.
9. Regular electronic contact with the distance learner is most essential

even if only to chivvy and encourage. Response times need to be kept to a few days, unless one of the parties is away from their base. Each party needs to kept informed, or better still consulted about, planned absences.

10. Commenting on written drafts needs to be done on a regular and frequent basis. This needs to occur at every stage of the student's writing-up phase, section by section or chapter by chapter.

11. Doctoral study for the distance learner does not have to be analogous to the 'loneliness of the long distance runner'. There are plenty of opportunities to create networks, learning communities and contacts – but these have to be nurtured and maintained and that includes the virtual learning environment (VLE) which many courses now employ. The VLE has to be maintained and 'kept alive', otherwise it will be ignored by distance learners who have a myriad of other things to do – students need an incentive and a reward for joining the learning community that a VLE can provide.

12. Face-to-face contact is still valuable and extremely important for the distance learner, even if it is expensive and time-consuming. It can, on occasion and if at all feasible, be fitted in around other travel being undertaken by student or supervisor.

13. Many, if not all, of the principles of good practice in supervising distance learners will apply equally to campus-based students, and vice versa.

13

An Issue of Teaching

Scenario

Max was an excellent student now in the second year of his PhD investigating the way local dialects had affected spoken English. His supervisor, Professor Green was very pleased with how well Max's research work was progressing. Because of his outstanding progress Professor Green thought it would be beneficial to Max to undertake some limited tutorial teaching. He duly approached his student with this suggestion, and Max, although a little unsure of his abilities to do this, accepted the idea with alacrity. Reflecting later after his teaching, Max realized he had really enjoyed the experience and thought it could well be extremely useful and relevant for him should he decide to pursue an academic career.

Points for Consideration

- What are the advantages to the student in undertaking some teaching duties while they are researching full-time?
- What are the disadvantages?

Not surprisingly, at the beginning of Max's third year, he was again asked if he would like to take tutorial sessions in the first semester. Max enthusiastically agreed to do so, but found the sessions, and the preparation for them, quite time-consuming and was relieved when the sessions had finished. He was keen to complete a really good PhD in three years, and felt these teaching duties had eroded the time he needed for his research.

However, at the beginning of the second semester, Professor Green, who was a keen squash player, had a heart attack on the squash court and was advised not to return to work for several weeks. This caused a major problem and posed a real dilemma for the department as the Professor was about to teach his core module to final-year undergraduate students and no other member of staff really had the expertise to teach the module. Moreover, the department was already stretched as several academics were on sabbatical desperately trying to increase their chances of promotion and increase their departmental Research Assessment Exercise (RAE) rating. A possible solution was to enquire if an English specialist from the other university in the same city would be able to step in at short notice. However, the lady concerned was herself about to spend time at an overseas university and therefore could not oblige.

In desperation, the Head of Department thought that Max might well be the solution. His area of expertise was perfect and he already had teaching experience. So Max was approached. Admittedly he felt flattered but he really didn't want to do it. However, how could he let the Head of Department down when the situation was critical, and especially when the latter had offered to become his supervisor in Professor Green's absence? Moreover, it was possible that, career-wise, a refusal might not be looked upon favourably. So he accepted.

Points for Consideration

- Should any research student be asked to contribute to a significant part of the departmental teaching load under any circumstances?
- Is it a good idea for a student to be expected to teach a module without any apparent training?
- Could a case be made for allowing capable graduate research students to take on some limited teaching duties under critical circumstances?
- Should a research student's career prospects be influenced by decisions he might take about departmental academic matters and requests?

There was little time for preparation and Max was under considerable pressure to deliver, which, on the whole, he did at a satisfactory level. However, Max experienced some unexpected difficulty with one of the students taking the module, and who failed to respect his authority. This led to some antagonism between Max and the student. The examination for this module followed shortly after the module was completed, and the contretemps came to a head when the student was found to have failed the module, and gained only an upper second class degree, where a first had been expected. Unfortunately for Max, and the department, the student appealed against the degree decision, citing Max's teaching incompetence in that particular module as one of the reasons for his upper second degree.

With the Head of Department's help, Max was soon able to return on track to his research work which continued to progress, although much more slowly than before, but both Max and his Head of Department were pleased with Max's module teaching efforts, until news came through about the final year student's degree and his appeal against it, especially when the appeal was upheld. The department became embroiled in various ramifications associated with this appeal, naturally involving Max, who found the whole situation difficult to accept, and it developed into a traumatic time for him as he thought it could have a damaging effect on what had started to look like the promising beginnings of an academic career.

What had originally been a well-planned third year of PhD study now turned into one that was beginning to look short of time, and this considerably exacerbated Max's feelings of unease and concern. Unfortunately, all this added up to a continuation of his research into a fourth year which further added to Max's frustration and despondency.

Eventually, Max's supervisor, Professor Green, returned to work, succeeded in inspiring Max, got him back on track again, and the thesis was duly completed and successfully defended at the *viva* examination towards the end of year four.

Points for Consideration

- How might the effects of these disrupting events on the student and his research progress, have been minimized?
- Is the research student in a position to lodge a formal complaint about his difficulties?
- Would it be in the student's best interest to do so?

Evolution of the problem

The student should not have been asked to make a major contribution to departmental teaching, whatever the circumstances. It is obvious that the demands on the student's time would be considerable and might seriously disadvantage him. On the other hand, the advantages of having done some limited experience of teaching could be used by the student in certain job applications.

Unfortunately, it was too easy for the Head of Department to ask a research student to help out with the teaching, as the student would have found it difficult to refuse, and as indicated above, the student could perceive advantages for his immediate career in the opportunity.

The responsibility and time involved in delivering a complete teaching module are an excessive demand on a student, even an extremely capable one, and are of a very different order from delivering the odd tutorial. There are also very different obligations that a student has to meet in a third year, as compared to the second year, of a PhD research programme.

It is unlikely, although not impossible, that the Head of Department would hold it against a graduate research student if he decided not to help out with a specific task in a crisis. However, this is immaterial as the student will not perceive it this way, and will, by the very nature of things, assume the opposite.

There is no indication that the student had any training for the module teaching role he was asked to undertake, and with little time available for preparation, the student, placed in a difficult position, would be very hard put to be entirely successful in his efforts.

It is surprising that a busy Head of Department would be in a position to provide any significant help to the student with his research work. It appears that the student's research progressed less than satisfactorily in the absence of his supervisor.

There is no mention of the graduate research student seeking help and advice from a teaching mentor when he encountered difficulties with one undergraduate student in particular. The student also failed to seek assistance from those members of the department's staff who might have been available.

Possible prevention and resolution of the problem

1. The expectations of a student to contribute to teaching should be reasonable and clear, and any student who is asked to contribute to teaching should have the tasks outlined in writing.
2. A student who will be teaching should have the appropriate training for the task and be allocated an appropriate, experienced member of the academic staff as a mentor.
3. The Head of Department should have found an alternative solution to the teaching problem; this could have been as extreme as dropping the module from the final year undergraduate teaching programme altogether.
4. Although the Head of Department offered to help the student in the supervisor's absence, additional help such as that from a Graduate Tutor might have been of considerable value.
5. Because of the difficulties experienced in the teaching of the final year undergraduate module, the department might have taken steps to minimize the contributions that this module might make to the examination papers, or at the very least, have alerted the relevant Examination Board as to the situation regarding the teaching of this module.

14

An Issue of Management

Scenario

Although Dr James Angus, Reader for 12 years in the Department of Reproductive Medicine at Kettleborough University, had many publications to his name, his most recent was four years ago. At the request of his Departmental Head, he'd agreed, 18 months previously, to supervise Angela, who had scraped a 2.1 degree in Molecular Biology, for an MPhil/PhD. Dr Angus felt obliged to take on this supervision; he had no other graduate students, and three years would take him to his retirement. There was also the Triennial 'Population and Fertility' Conference in Bermuda in three years time to consider.

Points for Consideration

- As an older staff member with no recent publications, are the motivation and commitment of the supervisor questionable?
- Is the Head of Department wise in requesting the supervisor to accept the student?

In spite of the relatively poor quality of Angela's first degree, she had made some progress with her research during the first year, although during that time, she had missed a couple of research progress discussions with Dr Angus, and her departmental research talk had been notable only for the extremely nervous manner in which Angela had delivered it. Just after her talk, Dr Angus had been unable to contact Angela for three weeks. However, he'd given her a good 'talking to' when she finally reappeared, and decided she'd made just about enough progress to warrant transfer to a PhD despite her poor research presentation. Her transfer to the PhD programme was supported by an academic panel who also considered that she had just about done enough. As all six of the department's MPhil students achieved transfer with no apparent difficulty, the Head of Department was certain that management of research students was being carried out successfully.

Points for Consideration

- Is it possible that the capabilities, commitment and temperament of this student are not up to undertaking a PhD degree?
- Could there be a personality mismatch between supervisor and student?

In her second year Angela's research progressed slowly. Over the first three months she had three meetings with Dr Angus during which it seemed to her that he spent most of the time stressing the need for rapid progress, delivering 'pep talks', and indicating most forcibly that one particular element of the research she was currently engaged on could 'make or break' her PhD. Since then, however, Dr Angus, under some pressure with teaching duties, had hardly seen Angela, and although he'd tried to contact her through messages and e-mail, three of their monthly meetings had been missed and Angela had not responded to his attempts at contact.

Points for Consideration

- Where does the fault for the unproductive meetings between student and supervisor lie?
- What is the reason for the breakdown in communications?
- What is wrong with the management of this research project and who might be at fault for this?
- Could the situation have been recognized earlier and, if so, by whom?

Then, early in April of her second year, Angela requested an urgent meeting with Dr Angus. From the outset of the meeting, Dr Angus could see Angela was nervous and upset. Almost in tears, she soon informed him that she was very unhappy with the work, felt unable to cope with even the most straightforward parts of her research programme, and that the important experimentation, central to her research, was simply not working. In any case she couldn't see it producing the necessary novel results Dr Angus had suggested it would. Dr Angus told her not to be silly, that she was getting all 'het up' and that the way through this was to repeat the experiments again as soon as possible. Angela's response to this, however, was to burst into tears, and through her sobs said she'd heard Dr Angus's previous graduate student had withdrawn in his final year without submitting his thesis, and that she wanted to change to another supervisor! Just as Dr Angus, now becoming quite angry, was about to reply, his telephone rang. On the line was his Head of Department who had just opened a letter from Angela saying she couldn't cope with her research and wished to withdraw from her PhD. What the hell was going on? Could Dr Angus come and see him immediately?

Points for Consideration

- Why is the student failing to cope with her research work?
- Is the research work itself part of the problem here – is the project a viable one?
- What are the possible reasons behind the student's loss of confidence in her supervisor?
- Are the student's expectations of research work unrealistic and, if so, what might be the reasons for this?
- Is the commitment of both supervisor and student to this project all it should be?
- Could the student have been handled more sympathetically when matters came to a head?
- Overall, how might this project have been better managed?

Evolution of the problem

The Head of Department was unwise to put pressure on a supervisor, who should have been recognized as being at a stage in his career where he might prove unsuitable as a supervisor, to accept a student, particularly a student who might well be lacking in research capabilities.

The supervisor is probably 'winding down' his research programme prior to his retirement, and his reasons for accepting the student are questionable. The supervisor's motivation may also not be all it should be, as his mind may not be fully focused on the requirements of the student.

It should have been recognized that the student was probably less than suitable to undertake a higher degree research programme, in terms of her intellectual capabilities, her understanding of the nature of research, and her commitment to research work.

The supervisor failed to establish a good, open working relationship with the student and, partly because of this, did not recognize the capabilities and limitations of the student, which in turn did not allow him to provide the assistance the student required. As a result, the student lost confidence in both her research programme and her supervisor, and failed to maintain the essential communication between them.

The widely differing temperaments of student and supervisor did not augur well for the establishment of a good working relationship between them. The student was primarily at fault for the loss of communication, but the poor management of the research programme, and the unhelpful research meetings between student and supervisor may well have contributed to student loss of confidence and research progress.

The student's situation should have been recognized at the time of transfer, but the good progress of all other students made a positive scenario for the department, while permitting all students to transfer to a PhD programme avoided potentially difficult and drawn-out problems and made for 'an easy life' for the departmental staff.

The action of the student in informing the Head of Department of her wish to withdraw from her PhD was precipitate, while the 'crisis' meeting between the supervisor and the student was badly handled by both.

Possible prevention and resolution of the problem

1. A more enlightened student selection procedure is required, and more consideration should be given in allocating students to specific supervisors.
2. The supervisor should have established a better working relationship with the student during her first year and managed the student and her research work with greater insight and sympathy throughout. This could have enabled the supervisor to recognize the nature of the student's problems earlier and taken steps to rectify them, or to at least ensure that an apropriate decision was made at the time of the transfer process.
3. There must be an immediate and constructive discussion between the departmental Graduate Tutor, the Head of Department, the supervisor and the student to resolve the situation, and attempt to build up the confidence of the student.
4. Depending on the perceived situation of the student's research work progress, the appointment of a mentor, or a second supervisor may be appropriate. Alternatively, it may be wise to advise the student to only submit for an MPhil degree. Withdrawal from the PhD probably represents the least suitable option for both the student and the department.

15

An Issue of Culture

Scenario

Dr Kevin Murray was keen to expand his research on wastewater manage-ment and, as luck would have it, he had received an application from an overseas student, Mustafa, who was interested in his research field. Dr Murray had never supervised an overseas student before and was slightly apprehen-sive about it. However, he knew Mustafa's governmental sponsor would make a significant contribution to the cost of the research and that was very attrac-tive. When Mustafa duly arrived at the start of the semester, Dr Murray was pleased that Mustafa appeared very competent in English and also his general attitude to work was very positive. He seemed very highly motivated and very anxious to please Dr Murray. During that first year all went well, Mustafa took note of everything that his supervisor said to him and he was well prepared for his MPhil/PhD transfer.

Points for Consideration

- Are the motives for taking on this student appropriate?
- What other factor(s) might the supervisor take into consideration in determining the suitability of this student?
- How might the supervisor obtain information about any specific problems associated with the supervision of overseas students?
- Should a supervisor treat an overseas MPhil/PhD student in any way differently from a home-based student undertaking an MPhil/PhD?

At the transfer interview, however, Mustafa did not perform as well as his supervisor might have expected. He perfectly described in great detail what he had done in his research, but on the other hand, struggled when asked questions as to why he had used particular methodologies, and what he understood by, and how he interpreted his findings. Consequently, at the end of the interview, the transfer panel had some reservations about his performance and about recommending his transfer. On balance, however, they considered that perhaps it was his understanding of English that had not helped him handle some of their intricate questioning, but it was the glowing report by Dr Murray, on Mustafa's research abilities and progress, that finally persuaded the panel to approve the transfer. Following the transfer, Dr Murray was happy for Mustafa to take an extended break back in his own country to see his family and friends.

Points for Consideration

- Is the natural tendency during the transfer process to give students the benefit of the doubt of real benefit to either the student or the supervisor?
- Could the transfer be delayed, the student advised on his shortcomings, and on how to reach a satisfactory level of research achievement and an understanding of the process of research?
- Also, could the supervisor be appraised fully of the student's situation, as perceived by the transfer panel?

On Mustafa's return, Dr Murray carefully explained what the plans were for his research during the next academic year and asked Mustafa to carry out some literature searches, so he could familiarize himself with this new branch of his research. For his part, although Mustafa partly understood what his supervisor had described to him, he remained somewhat at sea, and even failed to grasp some of the key points about the work. However, he felt he could not ask Dr Murray to explain the new work once again for him, and in more detail. Over the next few weeks, Dr Murray was away on paternity leave and when he did finally see Mustafa again, it was a very brief meeting as Dr Murray was trying to catch up on his teaching. He asked Mustafa if he had been able to start work on the new line of experimental research following his extensive reading, and although Mustafa really wasn't sure what he was supposed to be doing, his instinct to please meant that he was unable to say no, otherwise he would incur the displeasure of his supervisor and bring shame on himself. During the following few weeks, Dr Murray remained extremely busy but managed at times to ask Mustafa if all was going well with his research. Mustafa told his supervisor that everything was fine and that the work was progressing nicely.

Points for Consideration

- Even though the supervisor had other pressures to deal with, should he have left the student to look after himself?
- If the supervisor was not informed of the detailed opinions of the transfer panel, how might this affect his perception of the student's capabilities?

About a week following his last brief contact with Mustafa, Dr Murray received a message that his Head of Department wished to see him urgently. When Dr Murray arrived in the Head of Department's office, he was immediately asked what Mustafa was doing performing highly dangerous experiments using noxious chemicals. Dr Murray was stunned. He knew what Mustafa should have been doing but because he had been very busy of late, he had not personally observed the new work. It was a very red-faced and worried Dr Murray who went to find Mustafa immediately and asked him what on earth he had been up to. Mustafa was happy to explain the experiments to his supervisor, and Dr Murray then realized that what the Head of Department had said was true; his student was indeed engaged in work involving potentially dangerous substances, and in experiments that were not exactly what Dr Murray had proposed. Dr Murray was baffled. Why had Mustafa made such a series of serious mistakes? Why hadn't he come to ask for advice if he was unsure of what he was doing? Dr Murray asked Mustafa these questions, but failed to obtain answers he could make sense of. He was now concerned that maybe he shouldn't have taken on Mustafa in the first place, and he felt he had lost confidence in Mustafa's work. In a fit of temper, Dr Murray told his student his views, and also indicated that no way would Mustafa succeed with his PhD if he carried on as he had done over the last few months. Mustafa became extremely upset, and felt demeaned by his supervisor's outburst, and what his supervisor must think of his abilities. In addition, unbeknown to his supervisor, Mustafa faced considerable financial penalties and loss of face if he failed to return home to his country without a PhD degree, and Dr Murray's suggestion that he might fail or not gain a PhD was a grave worry for Mustafa and was the cause of many a sleepless night until Mustafa's research work was back on track.

Points for Consideration

- Should supervisors be made aware of any conditions placed on students, especially if they return to their home country without the degree for which they registered?
- If so, would academic judgement be affected?

Evolution of the problem

A lack of awareness of the varying needs of individual students and of the differences in cultural backgrounds, including possible different perceptions of authority figures such as supervisors, could potentially result in the exacerbation of any problems and unwittingly increase unhelpful pressures on the student.

Financial pressures may have affected academic judgement at the application stage, while apparent competence in English language does not always equate with comprehensive understanding.

Doubts raised by a transfer interview panel about the suitability of student transfer were ignored, due either to unwillingness on the part of the interview panel to transmit the information to the supervisor or to supervisor intransigence, or both. Students who cannot fully understand their work should have their transfer delayed. Apart from some weaknesses in English language, overseas students may have been educated in an unquestioning environment. This may not be a problem at undergraduate level but could pose difficulties in postgraduate research studies.

The student failed to clarify the nature and detail of his next piece of research work with his supervisor, perhaps due to cultural background. Also perhaps due in part to cultural background, the student misled his supervisor over the progress of his research.

The supervisor could have sought temporary supervision for the student even though it was only needed for a few weeks.

Possible prevention and resolution of the problem

1. The supervisor might benefit by attending a development (training) course which deals with those problems that can be associated specifically with international students.
2. It would have been advisable for the supervisor to have asked the Graduate Tutor or an experienced colleague to comment on the suitability of the student, as evidenced by the latter's application form and any other written information or contact the supervisor has had with the student.
3. The transfer panel might have been more forceful and decisive in their contact with the supervisor, who in his turn should have listened more carefully to the panel's views, after their interview with the student. A decision to postpone the transfer for two to three months might have allowed the supervisor time to resolve the situation.
4. The supervisor has to establish ways, and spend time getting the student to explain his understanding of the research work he is doing, as, because of cultural differences, he may be less likely to ask questions than other students. This could be done by asking for written pieces of work and/or requesting presentations of the student's research findings at regular intervals.
5. The student might benefit by attending advanced English language training in specific areas such as thesis writing and/or oral presentations.
6. For the student to feel, and to take, ownership of his research work, the supervisor should ask for written descriptions of the future research work

that the student thinks is appropriate. A greater involvement of time, and frequent feedback from the supervisor are then required.

7. The student should be reminded of what a supervisor's expectations are of a research student in the United Kingdom and how he needs to respond accordingly. This could be the responsibility of the Graduate Tutor.

16

An Issue of Funding

Scenario

Dr Parry was delighted to have been awarded a local NHS two-year grant to pursue his research work on osteoporosis. It would at least mean that he would have a pair of hands to do the laboratory work while he concentrated on his patients and the clinical aspects of his work. Of course, a total of two years funding would mean that he could offer a research assistant only the chance to submit the work for an MPhil degree. However, he had heard from colleagues that if he offered the work as a PhD project instead, he was likely to get better quality applicants. It wouldn't matter at this stage that he hadn't yet secured funding for the third year as he was fairly sure he could obtain that later on. Dr Parry therefore proudly offered a research assistantship in his laboratory leading toward a PhD.

Point for Consideration

- Can a student be registered for a PhD without the necessary financial support being available?

Jenny had just been awarded a first-class degree from a top quality university and had the pick of several research assistantships. However, she was particularly interested in Dr Parry's project as there had been a history of osteoporosis in Jenny's family and she really wanted the opportunity to make a contribution in this field. She applied for the post, was accepted and duly registered with the university which encompassed Dr Parry's Medical School, for an MPhil/PhD degree.

Points for Consideration

- Is it legitimate to advertise a financially unsecured position either on the open market or else internally in the institution?
- Should there be more clarity about what students are to be offered financially when applying for research studentships or assistantships?

In the first year Jenny and Dr Parry had an excellent working relationship. Dr Parry was busy of course, but made a special effort to obtain for his student as much clinical material from his patients as he possibly could. In return, Jenny had developed an excellent insight into the research involved, and worked both efficiently and seemingly tirelessly in the laboratory. Not surprisingly, Jenny's first year progress was excellent and her transfer procedure proved to be a mere formality. As a consequence of his student's dedication and excellent research work, Dr Parry was actively planning presentations at international conferences as well as publication of their work in high impact factor journals.

About six weeks after Jenny's successful transfer from MPhil to PhD, she contacted the laboratory manager about placing a large order for consumables to underpin her laboratory work over the next few months, as her research had been going so well. During a conversation with the laboratory manager, however, Jenny was asked where the funding was coming from for the third and final year of her project as Dr Parry's grant ran out at the end of the second year. Jenny was certainly taken aback by this news but felt that the laboratory manager must have made a mistake. Dr Parry had never mentioned that her PhD project was only funded for two years and she couldn't believe that he wouldn't have told her.

Point for Consideration

- Is it possible for a supervisor to conceal the truth about the finances available for an MPhil/PhD degree for so long?

Nevertheless, she thought she had better mention it to him so he could confirm that all was well. When Jenny approached Dr Parry, however, he became quite angry. Jenny had never seen him behave like this and he shocked her by saying that financial matters were not her concern and that she had no business asking him questions of this nature. However, he did admit, with a very bad grace, that her project did only have funding for two years, and on hearing this, Jenny was distraught.

Point for Consideration

- Was the student acting correctly in directly approaching her supervisor and asking him financial questions?

A couple of days later, Dr Parry, having had time to think about Jenny's situation, asked to meet her. Jenny was not looking forward to seeing Dr Parry but he did apologize to her for his behaviour. He pointed out that he had always intended to pursue funding for the third year but had been so busy over the past few months that he had just not got around to doing it. Unfortunately, he was about to start an intensive period of clinical teaching for several weeks, on top of his regular clinical commitments, and would over that period be unable to devote any time to sorting out the required funding. He told Jenny that he thought the best way forward might be for her to submit several applications for funding to pharmaceutical bodies. Jenny agreed to try this, as after all, her future depended on it, but she did not have this sort of experience, and despite several worthy attempts, no funding was forthcoming.

Points for Consideration

- Should students be writing grant applications to help provide funding for their research work?
- Should the writing and preparation of applications for funding form part of the training for graduate students?

Several months passed and Jenny was no nearer obtaining funding for the final year of her research project. Dr Parry had submitted a couple of grant applications recently but these were both for substantial sums and neither involved Jenny.

In his discussions with his student, Dr Parry always expressed good intentions but these failed to materialize into anything substantial or financially helpful to Jenny and not surprisingly, these financial matters were putting quite a strain on their working relationship. Feeling sick with worry, and almost desperate, Jenny went to Dr Parry's Head of Department to ask if he could help out. He was rather shocked to hear the story and he reassured Jenny that the department would do all it could to set the matter right.

Point for Consideration

- Although the Head of Department was sympathetic towards the student's predicament, has the department any responsibility towards solving the problem?

Dr Parry was annoyed at Jenny for going to his Head of Department but he did after some effort, manage to raise sufficient monies to cover the laboratory consumables and tuition fees that would be required for Jenny's final year. However, he was unable to raise any funding to cover Jenny's maintenance fees. It was, however, in his mind, that as Jenny was such a competent student, and that he had, after all, managed to obtain some funding for her project, he felt able to suggest to her that she should cover her own maintenance by working part-time. In any case many students worked to pay themselves through university, so this wasn't really any big deal.

Point for Consideration

- Is it reasonable that students be asked to work part-time to help support themselves financially?

In some ways Jenny was relieved that her PhD research project had been saved but she was very disappointed that Dr Parry expected her to work part-time as well as doing her PhD full-time. Jenny's third year turned out to be a difficult one, and her research studies advanced more slowly. In addition, her working relationship with Dr Parry remained very strained, and, to make matters worse, her supervisor failed to understand why Jenny's progress was not as good as it had been before over the first two years. Jenny felt heavily pressured in her research work, and her supervisor was also coming under considerable pressure to publish the interesting new findings they had made earlier, but that now required confirmatory experimentation.

Point for Consideration

- Under the changed circumstances, were the supervisor's expectations still reasonable?

So despite Jenny being an excellent student, the pressure from her supervisor in the third year and the part-time work she had been forced to undertake, led her to seek counselling. As a result of these difficulties, Jenny had to carry her research experimentation on into a fourth year, and she only just managed to meet the four-year submission deadline for her PhD thesis. In the end, things turned out to be successful, and Jenny was awarded her PhD, but overall it had not been an enjoyable experience for her and she never forgave her supervisor for keeping her in the dark about the funding arrangements.

Points for Consideration

- Should training in financial management be available for supervisors of graduate students?
- What might be the far-reaching implications of the bad experience an individual could receive as a graduate student?

Evolution of the problem

The supervisor should not have offered the project with funding for only 24 months as a PhD. In doing so, he was being totally dishonest towards the student. However, it is not illegal for such advertisements to be placed, either internally or on the open labour market.

The unfair and dishonest approach of the supervisor enabled the true financial situation to remain hidden from the student, who in turn had no inkling of any problem and therefore was unable to ask any questions.

The supervisor was too keen to reap the benefits of the student's work before sorting out the financial difficulties he had created. The welfare of the student was not his first priority.

The supervisor did not behave in a responsible manner when the student discovered his dishonesty towards her, and this, together with the improbity of the supervisor, resulted in a deterioration of their working relationship. As a consequence, the student, the research work itself, and the supervisor all faced problems.

In the United Kingdom, graduate students are not normally expected to support themselves through any stage of their PhD research programme by writing applications for funding, although this is common in other countries. Although promising and attempting to help, the department failed to solve the financial problems, and, in fact, had no obligation to the student to do so.

It was unethical for a supervisor to suggest that a student work part-time to support themselves, particularly so when a supervisor has been dishonest and unfair to the student. The supervisor should also have considered that the research work could suffer should a student be forced to engage in part-time outside employment when involved in full-time research.

There was no indication that the supervisor had received any formal training in managerial skills, particularly human resource management and financial management.

Possible prevention and resolution of the problem

1. The supervisor should have, if possible, secured funding for a third year before advertising the position as an MPhil/PhD. Failing that, and if his available funding was to commence on a specific date, the position should have been advertised as an MPhil.
2. The supervisor should have advised the student of the financial position immediately at interview, while informing the student he would be looking for funding for a third year.
3. The supervisor should prioritize work in such a way that the welfare of the student is constantly reviewed, as with a good-quality student this will help ensure the successful progress of the research work.
4. There are seminars or courses in some institutions to provide information on the more general aspects involved in the preparation and writing of grant applications. These are available for both academic staff, and for graduate students who may be considering a career in research.
5. In many situations, it is often possible for a large department to find some funding, perhaps as a loan from one pocket of money to another, to support a student with financial difficulties which are not of their own making.
6. Although under present circumstances graduate students in the United Kingdom are accepted for MPhil/PhD degrees on the understanding that funding is secure for this, many research graduate students will supplement their funding through some part-time employment. This should be frowned upon, especially during the student's final year, as the research work can be more intense then and part-time work may consume the student's time and energy.
7. Supervisors can benefit from attending courses in managerial skills and these are often run by universities and other research institutions.

17

An Issue of Appeal

Scenario

John Stephens had been awarded a good first degree although he had had a few run-ins with his project supervisor in his final year, spoiling what had initially been a good working relationship. John was absolutely sure when he had finished his degree that he needed work experience, and it was a couple of years after graduation that he applied for a studentship to study with Dr Pratt with the aim of developing his research expertise in contemporary German poetry.

Perhaps rather unfortunately for Dr Pratt, there was a family bereavement just before the interviews for the studentship and this prevented her from being quite as thorough in the way she took up references. Nevertheless, John performed well at interview and Dr Pratt was pleased to offer him the position, which he duly accepted.

Points for Consideration

- What are the prime requirements in making an appointment of this nature?
- What do you consider to be the relative importance of the available references?
- How might the supervisor have better dealt with her work situation in the face of a sudden and unexpected absence?

The first year of John's research went well and he was in a strong position, enabling him to transfer from MPhil to PhD without difficulty. During the second year Dr Pratt and John were quite enthused about how the research was progressing and all looked well for the future.

About this time, however, John became embroiled in a difficult personal relationship which had a significant effect on his behaviour. He became moody and unpredictable and Dr Pratt wasn't really sure what was happening.

For a period of several months the mood swings continued and John's work took a nosedive. He failed to turn up for meetings and missed deadlines. Perhaps worst of all, John failed to explain to Dr Pratt what was going on, and in despair, Dr Pratt decided to discuss the matter with the Graduate Tutor to see what should be done next. The tutor decided it was imperative to seek a meeting with John to try to find out what the problem was.

After several attempts trying to contact John both at his home and in work, the Graduate Tutor finally caught up with him and was able to arrange a meeting between the two of them and the supervisor. John did not appear to be in a particularly good mood at the meeting, but the Graduate Tutor was able to get him to admit he had been experiencing a difficult time in a relationship, although things seemed a little more stable now.

During the course of the meeting, however, John claimed that what was really annoying him was that Dr Pratt, having indicated that she might want him to present some of his research work at a forthcoming major international conference, had then failed to inform him of the dates of this conference, and it was now far too late for him to make his arrangements to travel to, and attend the meeting. He had also spent quite a bit of time over the past few weeks in preparing a presentation for the conference, and not once had Dr Pratt asked to see it; as far as John was concerned, this had all been wasted time.

Points for Consideration

- How might a supervisor handle a problem arising in the private life of a student, particularly a mature student, when that problem is adversely affecting the research work?
- Could the meeting have been more constructive if the supervisor had not been present?
- Could the situation have been handled in a more appropriate way by the Graduate Tutor?
- Is the supervisor at fault here in not informing the student?
- Is the student using the issue as an excuse to complain, and as a cover for his own current shortcomings and lack of progress?

John just wouldn't let this matter go away and irrespective of how many times Dr Pratt tried to explain her reasons as to why she had been unable to make contact with John about the conference, it just seemed to make the problem worse. John seemed to think that he should be Dr Pratt's number one priority. For her part, Dr Pratt indicated that she considered John's research progress over recent months had been extremely poor, and it was clear to the Graduate Tutor that John's working relationship with his supervisor had all but broken down. In spite of this, when the Graduate Tutor asked John about his future, John was adamant that he wanted the PhD come what may. However, among the difficulties now facing them was that Dr Pratt remained very unhappy with John's lack of progress and had previously informed him that she considered perhaps the best solution was for John to leave on the grounds of insufficient progress. She had made it clear to him that if he would not go voluntarily, then university procedures would be put in place to exclude him from his studies. The meeting ended unsatisfactorily, and it appeared to all involved that this situation could not be resolved easily.

About two weeks later John received a letter from the university authorities informing him that measures were underway to terminate his registration due to inadequate research progress. He was, of course, livid, and was certainly prepared to lodge an appeal against such a decision. He considered that an appeal could be made on the grounds of poor supervision, and that he could certainly advance a good case for this.

Points for Consideration

- Has the supervisor followed the correct procedures?
- Could more have been done before the university authorities were called in?
- Should the university authorities have investigated the matter more thoroughly before taking their action?
- Should John's registration be terminated or should he be given a second chance?

Evolution of the problem

It is questionable whether the student was the right material for postgraduate research following his graduate project experience.

This case highlights the point that even with a very good working relationship between student and supervisor, personal problems can be very destructive. It also stresses what can happen due to lack of communication between the supervisor and student.

Under the circumstances, would it be appropriate for the student to have attended the conference anyway?

Given that the student may be open to a charge of irrational behaviour, the outcome of events might have been better if this could be conveyed in a sympathetic and constructive manner to the student.

The supervisor's actions may be considered to have been somewhat hasty, possibly due to the pressures she herself was experiencing.

The Graduate Tutor was unable to resolve the problem. This could be due, at least in part, to his failing to spend enough time on the matter, his failure to see the situation as thoroughly as he might have, or due to an inherent ineffectuality.

Should the student have been prevented from lodging an appeal? What are the rules/regulations of appeal?

Possible prevention and resolution of the problem

1. To improve student selection there might be a need for more structure of interviews so that particular types of information about the student can be obtained.
2. A second or co-supervisor might have been invaluable in attempting to keep a working relationship between the student and supervisor and/or give a second opinion on developments.
3. It might be advantageous at certain times to delay the start of a student-ship so that time can be gained to obtain references and hold interviews; funding bodies are often sympathetic in these situations.
4. With regular supervisory meetings, perhaps John's problems could have been identified sooner and professional counselling could have been an option.
5. With the breakdown in the working relationship, perhaps another super-visor (possibly a second or co-supervisor) could have taken over as lead.
6. The Graduate Tutor could have been more diligent and positive, and should be aware of the rules, regulations and procedures that should be followed in situations of this nature.

18

An Issue of Stability

Scenario

Daniel was over the moon when he discovered that the highly acclaimed physicist, Professor Warren, had accepted him as a research student to work on new developments in harvesting solar energy. However, Daniel, now in his second year, was becoming more and more frustrated as Professor Warren's absences from Lanchester University since his recent ground-breaking discovery on high temperature interactions between various solar flare micro-constituents, were increasing in length and frequency. Although Daniel had made good progress in his first year and had had no difficulties in achieving transfer to study for a PhD degree, over the past few months the number of meetings with his supervisor had dropped dramatically. Fortunately, funding for Daniel's work could not be better and overall departmental interest in his work was extremely encouraging. Nevertheless, Daniel was becoming frustrated as he felt he was losing both a sense of direction, and also confidence in his work. Normally, if a problem arose and he could not find Professor Warren he would consult the departmental Graduate Tutor but he was absent on long-term sick leave.

Points for Consideration

- Why might an extremely successful research academic in some ways not be the best choice of supervisor for a research student?
- What might the Head of Department and/or the departmental Graduate Tutor do to improve matters?
- Could security of funding in a research programme, and/or enthusiastic support from departmental colleagues and fellow students be allowed to compensate for lack of supervisor guidance?

A crisis point for Daniel was reached when he kept hearing rumours that

Professor Warren had been offered the prestigious directorship of the Energy Research Center in Texas, USA. Several weeks later Daniel received an e-mail from his supervisor informing him that he had accepted the new post in the USA. Professor Warren also stated in his e-mail that he hoped Daniel would continue to make progress in his research project but that another supervisor would have to be appointed, as it would not be possible for Professor Warren to supervise from across the Atlantic, and that it was also not possible for existing research students to transfer to the USA.

Points for Consideration

- Even though a supervisor is about to leave their present institution, should they break off all communications with their research students?
- If not, how might they manage the situation better?

On receiving the e-mail from Professor Warren, Daniel immediately made an appointment to see the Head of Department to enquire about a replacement supervisor. Unfortunately, the Head of Department had recently gone on a study visit to China, due to last six months, and instead Daniel was advised to meet with the Acting Head of Department who was frantically trying to submit a major grant application before the imminent deadline. At the meeting, which lasted only a few minutes, the Acting Head of Department was able to inform the student that Professor Warren had already let the department know he had been making excellent progress recently and there was nothing to worry about with regard to his PhD research studies in the immediate future. With this in mind, and as there would be a considerable time delay before a new supervisor could be identified, the department had decided that, as an interim measure, Dr Nigel Oxley, a Postdoctoral Fellow, appointed at the start of the previous semester, with some interest in Daniel's area of research, would be happy to oversee his work.

Point for Consideration

- What should the Acting Head of Department have done once he discovered that the supervisor was about to leave the institution?

Dr Oxley proved to be quite helpful to Daniel, even though he was without previous supervisory experience, and on the whole his working relationship with Daniel seemed to be very successful. All was well for about three months until, completely out of the blue, Dr Oxley informed Daniel he had accepted a lectureship in Ireland and would be leaving the university within the next month. Not surprisingly, Daniel was shocked to hear this news and immediately arranged a further meeting with the Acting Head of Department, who was able to tell him that as luck would have it a Visiting Academic from

Germany, a specialist in the area of research in which Daniel was involved, was expected to come to Lanchester in a few months time. However, Daniel was concerned and disappointed at this time delay, in addition to his worries over this further change in supervisor, particularly as his second-year progress talk was looming.

Points for Consideration

- Could the choice of a Postdoctoral Fellow as a temporary, replacement supervisor, be appropriate for this student?
- Are there any advantages to a student in a change of supervisor during the progress of a PhD research project?

At the second-year research progress talks departmental staff members expressed some criticism of Daniel's presentation regarding parts of his methodology, and also voiced reservations, as it appeared to them, concerning his lack of understanding of concepts with respect to one or two fundamental areas of his research. Daniel's situation at the presentations was not helped by Dr Oxley's failure to put in an appearance. After his talk, Daniel felt extremely fed up, irritated and depressed. It looked as though his initial good progress had now gone badly wrong, and this was not, he believed, through any fault of his, but because of the supervisory problems he had experienced over the past months. He would also be without any academic supervision in the near future just at the time when, he felt, he urgently needed it; he was really worried that his PhD work was losing its direction and momentum.

Points for Consideration

- Was it a good idea for the student to have presented his second-year research progress talk, given his present circumstances?
- What might be the possible effects on the student when his research progress is criticized?

Evolution of the problem

No second supervisor had been appointed for this research project, thus denying the student any immediate and supportive fallback position. No matter how good a student's progress has been through the first stages of his research work, there is no adequate substitute for good, direct and continuous one-to-one supervision throughout a PhD programme.

An acclaimed scientist whose supervisory interest wanes as his fame grows is not providing the best support to the student. The initial supervisor did not concern himself to find out how the student was progressing in his second year and should not have made disarming comments to the Acting Head of Department with regard to the student's progress.

Even though the working relationship may appear satisfactory to the individuals involved, a Postdoctoral Fellow will not have the necessary breadth of background to supervise a PhD student and is not a substitute for an experienced academic supervisor.

No deputy for the departmental Graduate Tutor with experience in dealing with student matters of this nature was available.

There was no exploration of any possible role that the initial supervisor may have played in continuing to give some guidance to the student, over just a short period of time, even though he was sited in another institution abroad.

Lack of continuity of supervision, and changes of supervisor during the progress of a PhD are most unsatisfactory. There was poor student management by the Acting Head of Department, and the problems with the student's research were pointed out to him at a time when he lacked the necessary advice, support and guidance.

Possible prevention and resolution of the problem

1. The department should have a policy in place that provides dual supervision for all graduate research students at the outset of their degree programmes. Such a policy will avoid the interim and unsatisfactory supervision by inexperienced Postdoctoral Research workers.
2. The acting Head of Department should have found a substitute for the departmental Graduate Tutor as soon as he became aware of his long-term sick leave.
3. There is no reason why the initial supervisor, even though he has decamped to the United States, should not have been asked (and be willing) to play some 'advisory' role to the student's research at least in the short term even while based abroad.
4. There must be an urgent meeting involving all concerned parties, including the student, with the Acting Head of Department to find the student a suitable supervisor from within the department who should, under the present circumstances, remain in place until completion of the student's PhD. If necessary, for subject expertise, it might also be useful to seek a supervisor external to the institution (possibly the Visiting Academic) who could provide guidance by e-mail and by occasional face-to-face meetings.
5. It would have made sense to postpone the student's research progress presentation, while, nevertheless, alerting the student to the fact that there were problems, until some support in the form of a new supervisor could be found. A replacement departmental Graduate Tutor could well

be involved in providing encouragement to the student and in explaining that the department had been remiss in its handling of the situation, but had now realized this and would be taking steps to remedy the situation as soon as possible.

19

An Issue of Ownership

Scenario

A mature, able and conscientious student, Anne-Marie was just completing the second year of her PhD, concerned with the ethics of community and rehabilitation, at the University of Whytton. Over the last seven months of her second year, Anne-Marie had carried out a series of studies at the behest of her supervisor, the Head of the Community Relations Section of the Division of Social Sciences, Professor Grant. Over this time period, due to a two-month sabbatical in Florida, various conferences and a long vacation, Professor Grant had paid only fleeting visits to the section, and, on these occasions, had merely put his head round the door to check briefly with Anne-Marie, and his other students that things were going well, and had then disappeared again.

Points for Consideration

- Is there sufficient and frequent enough contact between the student and supervisor?
- How much latitude should students be allowed in developing their PhD research programme?

At their first formal supervisor–student research meeting on his return, and on discussing the data Anne-Marie had generated, it became clear to Professor Grant that his student had completed a well-conducted and exciting piece of research that had produced novel findings, and clearly warranted rapid publication. It was also clear to the Professor, that although originating from his initial suggestions, to produce these new data, Anne-Marie had needed to collaborate closely with, and receive considerable advice from one of his lecturer colleagues in another section within the Division. Furthermore, some of the data that had been generated, had been meticulously analysed and tabulated by a computer buff, a postgraduate student in that same section. It was also clear to the Professor that Anne-Marie had been instrumental both in initiating these collaborations, interpreting the results and had possessed the insight to realize the importance of the findings, and bring them to their extremely successful outcome.

Points for Consideration

- Why has this situation arisen?
- Has the student exceeded her responsibilities or is she right to follow her instincts as a researcher?
- At what point could she have informed her supervisor of the developments in her research work?
- To whom does the credit for these results primarily belong?

Following the meeting with Anne-Marie, her supervisor speedily produced a draft paper from the data she had generated, and gave it to Anne-Marie to ensure the methodology was correct, and to make any minor alterations that might be necessary prior to submitting it for publication. On finding it in her pigeon-hole, Anne-Marie was initially delighted with seeing her data so rapidly and expertly converted into a paper suitable for publication, but soon became concerned and then upset to see that the first named author on the paper was her supervisor, Professor Grant, while the second named author was her supervisor's colleague; Anne-Marie's name was placed third on the authorship list, while the name of the student from the Computer Section of the Division who had helped her and worked quite hard was placed fourth and last. Anne-Marie worried over this, but was essentially pleased to see the paper submitted for publication, as it would almost certainly represent valuable support for her PhD, and she consequently felt unwilling to voice her concerns over the authorship list to her supervisor.

Points for Consideration

- Is this course of action by the supervisor in the best interests of the student?
- Should the student be concerned about the author order on the manuscript?
- Has the student any redress following this kind of action?
- Is the supervisor entirely within his rights to 'appropriate' this work?
- Where do the limitations of the 'contract' between the supervisor and the student lie?

Evolution of the problem

The prolonged absence of the supervisor from the department and the lack of any formal meetings between student and supervisor over the relevant time period allowed the student to take the initiative in her research studies. The latitude allowed to students in progressing their research will differ in each individual case, and also as the research progresses from the initial to the later stages. As it turned out in the scenario described above, the consequences of student ability and initiative have proved very positive and useful, but with less able students the outcome may have been a complete waste of time, with many negative consequences for the progress of the PhD.

The student failed to provide her supervisor with information regarding the direction her work was taking, and she should have made every effort to achieve this, despite the infrequent presence of her supervisor in the section.

The supervisor failed to liaise sufficiently with the student as he prepared the data for publication and has not given the student appropriate recognition, either in direct support through involvement with the preparation of the paper for publication, and/or through appropriate co-authorship.

The student did not appreciate the potential choices or 'rights' available to her in this situation, and should ask her supervisor about the authorship list and its order to discover what reasons lie behind this. Most researchers would consider that the student has not received the rewards to which she felt she was entitled for the abilities and initiative she has shown and for the outcome of her endeavours.

Possible prevention and resolution of the problem

1. Regular and frequent contact and formal meetings, between student and supervisor, would have given ample opportunity for the student to inform the supervisor of any unusual developments in the progress of the research work. With present computer technology the supervisor would expect to be kept informed by e-mail.
2. The supervisor should show a more enlightened attitude to the career requirements of the student, and the needs of student recognition for their contribution to the research programme.
3. Students should be made aware of the valuable and important role they can play in a research programme and how this can influence their future career.
4. The student could have gained considerable benefit and experience in writing for publication, and for her thesis, if she had been asked to contribute more extensively to the preparation of the paper, in terms of reading relevant background material, converting the data into tables or illustrative interpretations and drawing appropriate conclusions.

5. If the student receives no satisfactory response or explanation regarding the authorship disposition, then a formal meeting with the supervisor, the other contributors to the research findings, and possibly also the Graduate Tutor or Head of Department, should be convened to discuss the proposed publication arrangements.

6. A high profile name at the head of the authorship list may give greater weight and credence to the publication, possibly giving support to its acceptance in a well-respected and widely read publication. In any case, as the initial idea for the research work was the supervisor's and as the senior worker involved, the supervisor's name would, of course, head the authorship list. If the student plans a career in the area of her current research, evidence of a working association with an eminent researcher in the field may benefit her future employment prospects. However, the contribution made by the student warrants greater recognition, and she needs to ensure her name is placed second, and not third, on the authorship list. If however, the student had also written the first draft of the paper, she may well have appeared as first author, with the supervisor, as is often the case in medicine and the sciences, appearing last.

7. The unwritten 'contract' between student and supervisor implies a mutually supportive interaction between the two persons involved. On the one hand, the student receives training in research methodology, and gains a PhD with career prospects in research as the end result. The supervisor has a research project, usually of great interest to him, carried out by an increasingly skilled, capable and developing research worker. The supervisor's rewards include boosted career prospects, publications, prospective eminence in the long term, and the enjoyment of overseeing the development of a graduate student into a capable research worker.

20

An Issue of Availability

Scenario

Annabel had just started the third year of her research programme on the efficacy of Health Service counselling procedures in seven local, well-to-do suburban areas surrounding the city, and this seemed to have progressed satisfactorily over the first 18 months. She had been transferred to a PhD without problems at the start of her second year, and over this last summer had been working partly from home using her 'state-of-the-art' computer, but nevertheless still having to travel to several of the regional district hospitals to conduct interviews. All this while, she was also busy with caring for her active and demanding 4-year-old daughter, and last year had taken on the secretarial duties of the local ladies lacrosse team. Because of these commitments, Annabel had to organize her time with meticulous detail, but had always managed to attend the monthly meetings to discuss progress with her supervisor, Dr Tom Stanton, despite the fact that this entailed two bus journeys from her home and having to risk her daughter collected from her pre-school group by her rather 'scatty' mother-in-law. Now however, Annabel was somewhat concerned and irritated that since the previous May, she had had no contact with her supervisor. Admittedly, Annabel had not needed to visit the university over this time and she had also managed a two-week holiday at Borromouth Spa in the middle of August.

Points for Consideration

- To what extent should a supervisor be aware of the personal circumstances of a graduate student?
- What are the special difficulties of a student not consistently working on site?
- Are monthly meetings sufficient during the first two years of a PhD research programme?

> • Should the frequency of the meetings be increased, decreased or left unchanged in the final year?

Towards the end of August, just after returning from her holiday, Annabel had found a somewhat terse e-mail from Dr Stanton stating that he would be away on vacation and at two conferences for 'six weeks or so'. A further e-mail at the end of September informed Annabel that Dr Stanton was back and would like to see her to discuss her progress and plan the 'final push' for her research programme. This disconcerted Annabel as she was becoming aware that the data she had gathered over the three to four months prior to her holiday were proving inadequate for the analyses she wished to carry out, and, furthermore, did not appear to be supporting the hypothesis she was testing. She had also had considerable difficulties gathering further data since her return from holiday, as lots of people were away, and her daughter had been at home for most of this time suffering from chickenpox, and requiring Annabel's almost constant attention. Annabel recognized that the final push that Dr Stanton required was dependent on at least a reasonably clear-cut result from the data, and this just didn't appear to be there!

Points for Consideration

- • How can the problems associated with prolonged lack of student–supervisor contact be avoided?
- • What, if anything, is wrong or inappropriate about the supervisor's approach to the student at this point in time?
- • Has the student acted responsibly over this time period?

Annabel found her brief meeting with her supervisor in the third week of September unsatisfactory. Dr Stanton, clearly short of time, had outlined the various reasons as to why it had been difficult fitting her into his busy time-table and external commitments, and faced with this information at the outset of their meeting, Annabel had felt unable to express her concerns over her work in any details, and in any case had scarcely been able to get a word in edgeways. Dr Stanton had gone on to say he thought she was coping well, that 'it sounds as though her work was well on track', and that 'in his experience a research student entering the final year of their PhD should be considered a competent research worker certainly able to solve any minor problems that might arise'. He had rapidly scanned through the data that Annabel had been able to show him, said they looked fine, and suggested he and Annabel should meet again towards the end of October, as she should have 'further amplified and clarified her data by then', and hopefully, he would have 'a little more time'.

Points for Consideration

- Is the supervisor's handling of this meeting to be commended?
- Are the supervisor's comments on the capabilities to be expected from a third-year PhD student realistic?
- Should the student have been able to manage the meeting in a way more useful to her?

Annabel went home feeling discouraged, concerned and a little panicky. After a week spent trying to get to grips with what she felt had to be done, she e-mailed and phoned her supervisor several times requesting an urgent meeting. She received no reply, but was informed by the departmental secretary that Dr Stanton was not available just at present, but she would pass a message on to him. Increasingly concerned about the block that appeared to have brought her work to an almost complete standstill, Annabel was still further dismayed by Dr Stanton's eventual e-mail to her. It was to the effect that due to his extremely busy teaching schedule, and a European Union research funding proposal on which he was working flat out to meet a late November deadline, their next research meeting would have to be postponed to the start of December at the very earliest.

Points for Consideration

- Is the supervisor misreading the capabilities of the student?
- What should the supervisor's priorities be?
- To what extent should a supervisor be at the 'beck and call' of a graduate student entering the third year of their PhD programme?

Annabel, who by now felt completely without direction and support, decided to take matters to the departmental head. On telephoning his secretary to make an appointment, however, she was informed he would be in Sweden for the next three weeks, but she would pencil in a date for a meeting with him if Annabel so wished. She also asked Annabel if there was anyone else who might help.

Points for Consideration

- Is this an appropriate strategy for the student to solve the problems that have arisen?
- What alternatives might be available to her?
- Who might be able to help her?

Evolution of the problem

A student working on a research programme based wholly or partially off campus, and with a busy and demanding home life is more likely to experience communication difficulties, and consequently may feel isolated.

A supervisor working under pressure with many work commitments may become overstretched, and consequently be relieved to accept a too cursory working relationship with one or more research students who are apparently making satisfactory progress.

The supervisor's expectations of the student were too high – either the situation in which the student was placed or the capabilities of the student, or both, were misjudged.

The period of the summer vacation may be the time when 'research matters may be left unattended and allowed to drift', albeit unintentionally, by both supervisor and student.

The student has been unable to make her concerns about the research work, and her progress, clear to her supervisor due to his misplaced priorities, his intransigence and his workload.

There was insufficient pertinent and 'in-depth' communication between the supervisor and the student at both the research work and personal levels, the fault lying primarily with the supervisor.

Possible prevention and resolution of the problem

1. The supervisor should be aware of the likelihood that a given student could be isolated from the mainstream research life of the department and should throughout the time of the research studentship make every attempt to ensure the student visits the department for any relevant working or social activities, and that there is no loss of regular contact with the student.
2. Once a supervisor has accepted a research student for a higher degree, then ensuring that the progress of that student is maintained to a successful conclusion should be a high priority for the supervisor, and they should both arrange their commitments and workload to take this into account.
3. Supervisors should always be aware that research work may present problems beyond the abilities of a student to solve alone, and may require the greater experience and expertise of the supervisor to resolve.
4. This situation is redeemable. The student should seek out the help and advice of the relevant Graduate Tutor (or their deputy if available), and also ensure that the Head of Department is made aware of her concerns and worries.
5. At the earliest possible opportunity, an informal meeting between the

Graduate Tutor, the supervisor and the student should be arranged to determine the way ahead. The outcome of this will depend on the state of the research work, primarily as perceived by the supervisor, and the possibilities of salvaging this.

6. Some work must be done on repairing the working relationship between the supervisor and the student. In most circumstances this can be done successfully.

7. The supervisor appears confident that the goal of a PhD is achievable for this student. Provided the working relationship can be improved, the supervisor needs to set up more communication with the student to move the work along, solve any real problems with the work and attempt to restore the confidence of the student.

21

An Issue of Health

Scenario

When she initially accepted Meg Francis, Dr Markham was confident that she would turn out to be a fine PhD student, as she had known her as her tutee, throughout Meg's undergraduate years. For her part too, Meg was very keen to pursue her studies in International Law at Greenbank University with Dr Markham. Over the first two years of the PhD, all had progressed smoothly and well, but in the January of the third year of the PhD, Meg was off ill for a couple of weeks with a suspected viral infection. Although Meg returned to her work for a further two weeks, she had to report to her GP again as she did not appear to be recovering at all quickly. After several weeks of continuing to feel unwell and a few more visits to the GP, Meg was finally diagnosed as having a post-viral, ME-like illness, a chronic disabling disease.

The next few months were a difficult time for Meg as she often did not feel well enough to undertake her studies at the university, and although Dr Markham was at first concerned about the lack of progress with Meg's work, her new appointment as Deputy Dean at the start of the semester occupied much of her thoughts and increasing amounts of her time. Not surprisingly, when the three-year period of PhD study was completed, Meg still had not finished her research work and was in no position to even consider writing-up.

Points for Consideration

- What options are open to the supervisor under the circumstances of a potentially long-term debilitating illness in a student in the latter stages of a PhD research programme?
- What other help can be obtained to support the student?

Over the next year, Dr Markham did make several attempts to arrange meetings with Meg, but her student had to cancel almost all of them due to persistent ill health, and the ones where they did manage to get together always lacked a feeling of drive and motivation, with Meg seeming just a shadow of her former, energetic self. Consequently, at the end of her fourth year, Meg was not much closer to writing-up than the year before and Dr Markham was not only beginning to lose interest in the project, but without any impetus from Meg, was now considering the possibility that the thesis might never be submitted.

At the end of the fifth year of her PhD, and having obtained a 12-month extension, Meg arranged a meeting with her supervisor to discuss the future of the work and possible submission of the thesis. Dr Markham was very concerned that Meg's research work was already looking rather dated in the light of several recent publications in her field of work. Her dilemma was, would Meg's PhD thesis now be acceptable? Her other major concern was whether Meg would ever be in a position to complete it anyway, as Meg would not be allowed to continue her PhD registration into the sixth year without permission of the Pro Vice-Chancellor and Dr Markham was in two minds whether to make the recommendation or not. At a meeting with Meg, Dr Markham suggested that it might be preferable to submit the existing work for an MPhil, rather than trying to finish what appeared to be an almost impossible task.

Points for Consideration

- Knowing that the effect might be demoralizing, was it right for the supervisor to warn the student that the topic of her research project was looking a little dated?
- Can a PhD become out-of-date before it is completed?
- In these circumstances, are the grounds for recommending downgrading to an MPhil justifiable?
- Should an MPhil ever be classed as a failure?

However, Meg was very upset at this, saying that despite her illness she had worked really hard during the last five years and was not prepared to throw it all up now for a 'worthless' MPhil. Dr Markham was quite concerned and disappointed at Meg's response, and asked her to go away, think carefully about what she had said, and to come back a week later so that a final decision could be made.

What was Dr Markham to do? She was unsure whether Meg had the commitment, or the capability, in view of her illness, to continue, but clearly Meg, at least as an immediate or instinctive reaction, did not wish to feel 'downgraded'. However, Dr Markham knew the long-standing illness was an important factor she must take into account in resolving the problem. As Deputy Dean this scenario was starting to become something of an embarrassment for her, and she would like to have the situation sorted out as quickly as possible. Meg was equally upset and wondered whether she could or should trust Dr Markham any longer, as she seemed reluctant to lend her the support Meg needed to enable her PhD to be brought to a successful conclusion.

Points for Consideration

- Is the 'downgrading' of the student to an MPhil the best way of resolving this problem?
- Why do you think the supervisor chose this option?

If Dr Markham was no longer going to support her PhD registration, when Meg really felt she could complete it, then what could she do? Perhaps she should submit a complaint against Dr Markham, or even appeal against what she thought would be an unjust decision if Dr Markham went ahead with her 'threats' as Meg perceived them.

Points for Consideration

- Is the student's proposed action in submitting a complaint, a justified one?
- Who is responsible for this situation reaching a breakdown point?

Evolution of the problem

When a PhD research programme is prolonged for whatever reason, but especially if it is due to ill health, it is often easier for the supervisor to adopt the line of least resistance and to allow the student leave of absence and/or extensions of study, than to confront the real source of the problem. In the scenario described here, it appears that leave of absence periods were not considered.

No special arrangements were made by the supervisor to try and create a more structured approach to project guidance and provide goals during the student's periods of absence.

In certain subject areas, the longer the PhD continues, the greater the chance that the research work can become out-dated.

An MPhil degree is often mistakenly regarded by students particularly, but also by some supervisors, to be a failure if the student's original registration was for a PhD degree.

No attempt was made by the supervisor to clarify/confirm the illness through a medical practitioner and the institution's health care facilities. No detailed records were kept of time away from the university. No medical certificates were provided by the student or requested by the supervisor.

Possible prevention and resolution of the problem

1. A medical practitioner's opinion should be sought with regard to the student's health, and the supervisor thoroughly appraised of the situation, to ensure that the student is well enough to study and continue with her PhD work and write-up.
2. It is suggested that in the circumstances, an appropriate and acceptable plan of action is created for the student, incorporating a detailed time-table including specific targets to be met over agreed time periods. Regular meetings should be arranged with the student, the supervisor, and another academic (either a co-supervisor or Graduate Tutor) and details recorded on a Meeting Log which is signed by all parties.
3. The supervisor should have been more pro-active in recording all formal meetings with the student. A more watchful eye should also be kept on students who are ill and detailed records kept of absences from university, including copies of medical certificates requested and provided. 'Problem' students should be discussed with the departmental Graduate Tutor for advice and the department informed as to what is going on. Such information provides a picture of the development of the situation, allowing decisions as to the outcome to be more readily and correctly made.
4. With the relationship between the supervisor and student in danger of breaking down, and to avert a difficult and potentially long-lasting problem, it is suggested that perhaps a co- or second supervisor could give another opinion as to the current validity of the PhD research work. This would help to determine decisions on the urgency required in completing the submission and point the way forward.
5. If the student can meet all the targets set, then one would imagine that she be allowed to submit for a PhD with a further possible extension granted and a note in the thesis explaining the reasons why some of the material presented may be out-dated. If it transpires that the student is making little effort to meet targets and complete the work, then as long as all records have been maintained, a recommendation should be made in writing to the student that submission for a PhD is no longer an option and that the work should be completed as soon as possible for submission towards an MPhil. It would also be in order to indicate a realistic, yet absolute deadline to the student for the MPhil submission to avoid a protracted timescale to the situation.

22

An Issue of Direction

Scenario

Alan was into the final year of his PhD in Sociological Computation at Yardborough University. The departmental staff, including his supervisor, regarded him as a potentially excellent researcher, highly motivated and intelligent, with drive, determination and an excellent grasp and appreciation of his work and its contribution to, and position in, a more generalized and wider, yet relevant, context. One paper stemming from Alan's work had already been accepted for publication in a good-quality journal, and he was currently occupied with the preparation of a second paper on another aspect of his research studies.

Point for Consideration

- Is it feasible or desirable to expect competent students, whose research work is progressing well and rapidly, to take time out to write and assemble their work for publication, during their PhD programme?

At a recent conference, Alan had met a Senior Lecturer in Computational Sociology from a neighbouring university. During their discussions, it had emerged that Alan could well undertake an interesting sideline to his research on a topic which appeared, at least to Alan, to fit in well with his existing research programme. Alan's initial enthusiasm about pursuing this extra work increased considerably when the Senior Lecturer mentioned the possibility of a post-doctoral position he hoped to have available in six months time on the very same topic, for which, he suggested, Alan might like to apply. On returning to his department at Yardborough University, Alan began to pursue this interesting line of research. It all looked very promising, and after almost two months of investigation, Alan had some very interesting preliminary data, but he recognized, with some concern, that further exploration and follow-up were still required.

Points for Consideration

- To what extent might a student consider following a research line without the specific approval of the supervisor?
- Should the student have contacted his supervisor prior to commencing this new direction of research?

Because of his supervisor's administrative and teaching duties, and attendance at conferences, Alan did not have a research meeting, or contact his supervisor over the subsequent two months. When a research meeting between them finally took place, in late April of his final year, Alan produced his preliminary data with a sense of excitement and expectation. To his complete surprise, however, his supervisor, having listened carefully to Alan's exposition, was vehemently against both the data that Alan had produced (in which she pointed out some methodological flaws unnoticed by Alan), and against the pursuit of the whole new direction of research. She predicted that, in her opinion, the approach could not lead to clear-cut and usable results if pursued further, as inherent in the approach was an untestable hypothesis. She also stated that she was unable to see how the approach could fit in with the research Alan had already completed, with the existing overall strategy of his research, or with his PhD presentation, saying that if it were to be included in his thesis it would seem almost like an added afterthought or an addendum, and the coherence of his research work to date could well be compromised.

Points for Consideration

- Why has the student failed to properly assess the value of this new direction of research and its relevance to his existing work?
- What contributory factors should a student expect a supervisor to bring to the progress and direction of a research programme?
- Why has this situation arisen, and who is at fault?
- Could this meeting have been handled differently by either the student or the supervisor?

Matters at this meeting with his supervisor became much worse when Alan revealed that the new line of direction for his research work had emerged following the discussions he had had with Dr Chris Hatton, the Senior Lecturer at Stadbrooke University. In the heat of the moment, Alan, although he had some misgivings about it in his mind, informed his supervisor in no uncertain terms that he thought he would be able to produce useful results from the work. Going through his mind was the wish to prove to his own satisfaction that the line of research could be worthwhile, to emphasize his research capabilities to his supervisor, and to demonstrate to her that she was not always right! From comments within the department, Alan believed he had already done enough work to get his PhD, and to successfully complete this further piece of research would increase his chances for a post-doctoral post either in his own or another department, and therefore it must be a good career move for him.

Points for Consideration

• Could a compromise have been reached at this meeting?
• Should either the student or the supervisor refuse any compromise?
• What does this meeting illustrate about the nature of the relationship between the student and supervisor?

At the end of the meeting Alan's supervisor curtly told him to go and read some of Dr Hatton's publications. She also informed Alan that she would not permit him to submit his thesis if he wanted to include the results of this extra research as, in her opinion, besides being unreliable and controversial, it would significantly alter her vision of his thesis in its final form. She informed Alan that she had successfully supervised eight students for their PhD degrees and her research experience in this area must be worth something and Alan should think about that. However, Alan took the view that his abilities were being questioned, remained hurt, annoyed and upset and he told his supervisor he would continue the research line, and write it up for inclusion in his thesis, without her approval if that was the way she felt, and then stormed, angrily, out of the room.

Points for Consideration

• How rigid should a supervisor be regarding the overall content and presentation of a PhD thesis?
• In the final year, to what extent should a student display and execute their research capabilities?
• Can a student submit a PhD without the approval of the supervisor?

Evolution of the problem

The student may be in difficulties over time, and is in danger of taking on too much work in the final year, with the thesis write-up, a paper being prepared for publication, plus a new research direction to be followed.

Even though a student is showing considerable promise as a competent and capable researcher, a major change of direction or new initiative in the research work should not be taken or followed without prior consultation with the supervisor.

Again, although students may appear extremely competent, they will not be experienced enough to detect potential problems or pitfalls in a novel research line, especially when the new approach or direction is made by someone who cannot be fully familiar with their existing work and overall research strategy.

The student has failed to appreciate and take advantage of the experience and expertise of the supervisor in this situation.

There was a lack of regular and formal research meetings between student and supervisor. This meant that the supervisor failed to monitor student progress effectively at a critical point in their research programme. Conversely, the student was over-confident in his abilities to the extent that he felt he could 'go it alone'.

If there was controversy, disagreement and dislike between academics involved in this situation (and this can occur at the cutting edge of research), then this should not have impinged on the student's PhD programme.

Over-confidence, as well as lack of confidence, in a student in their overall understanding of a research programme they are undertaking, can sometimes present a supervisor with problems.

There was no attempt by the supervisor to look for possible compromise in the alternative research pathways, and there was a lack of tact on the part of the supervisor in dealing with the student over this problem, although the timing of it (midway through the student's final year) will undoubtedly be a cause for supervisor concern.

Possible prevention and resolution of the problem

1. A student should always inform the supervisor of a proposed new direction for the research, but especially so at this late stage of the PhD research programme. The supervisor can then assess this not only for its own merits, but also in the context of the work already completed and the time available to the student for completion of the research and the thesis write-up. Discussions with peers and senior colleagues concerning research progress and direction is normally beneficial to young research workers.
2. Although over-confidence could be regarded as a valuable asset in a research student, when it leads to entrenched positions, to a failure to recognize priorities and to put a situation into perspective, then it is less than helpful. Students should recognize the expertise of their supervisors both in the research field and in their knowledge and experience in guiding them to a successful PhD submission.

3. Students should demonstrate a mature attitude and be aware of their limitations; the student should not lose sight of the fact that the PhD submission and its success are top priority.
4. The fault for this situation lies primarily with the student for the reasons outlined above. However, the supervisor's less than enlightened approach to dealing with the student also contributed to its deterioration.
5. Specifically, the supervisor should have maintained a closer contact with the student, managed her time more effectively, been more diplomatic and avoided confrontation about the situation at their meeting.
6. In view of the time constraints, as well as the supervisor's perception of the research compromising the new research direction (if justified), a compromise is not an option. As tactfully as possible, the student should be brought to realize the fallibility of his position. A less confident and more mature student would clearly have recognized this, but most likely would not have been in this position in the first place.
7. Maturity, understanding, experience and tact are all valuable assets in the student–supervisor relationship.
8. Supervisors should show flexibility and an openness to student suggestions (from whatever source) in their management of a PhD research programme, provided these are put forward in good time. The PhD programme is regarded, at least in part, as a training in research, and good, competent students would be expected to question, and sometimes differ from their supervisor's views, particularly in their final year.
9. In theory, a student can submit a PhD without the supervisor's approval although this would be regarded as most unwise. The Graduate Tutor and/or the Head of Department would be required to intervene and make decisions if the student and supervisor were unable to resolve their difficulties.

23

An Issue of Contract

Scenario

Anthony was nearing the end of the third year of his PhD programme, which had gone well under the supervision of Dr Veronica Good, and he felt he would easily be able to meet his end of September deadline for his PhD submission. In the middle of July, he'd given one draft results chapter to Dr Good which she'd not yet corrected and returned to him, and he'd left a further two results chapters with her secretary in the first week of August.

Anthony continued writing his remaining three chapters throughout August, happy that things were progressing smoothly, and eagerly looking forward to the exciting prospect of commencing the three year post-doctoral position he was due to take up in America the following January. In late August, as he was popping into the departmental library to check on some source references for this thesis, he unexpectedly bumped into Dr Good. 'Where are the last three results chapters you promised to get to me?', was her rather terse and snappy greeting. 'Don't you realize you've only about four weeks to go to your submission date, and you need to allow at least a week to get the thesis bound?' 'The writing is virtually done' Anthony replied, 'I'm just sharpening the chapters up a little, to get them just right. What do you think of the three chapters I've already given you?' 'They're all in your pigeonhole, and I'm afraid to say they all need considerable re-writing', responded Dr Good, adding quickly, 'I can't talk now as I've got a Faculty meeting to attend, but we must talk about them tomorrow and I do need the remaining chapters as soon as possible if you're to get your thesis in by the end of the month.'

Points for Consideration

- As it leads to increased pressure on both student and supervisor, is it wise for a student to accept a post-doctoral position before completing the thesis write-up?
- With a good and organized student, and an experienced supervisor working together, why might this last-minute crisis have arisen?
- What is the unwritten commitment entered into by both student and supervisor regarding the PhD?
- Are unexpected or hasty 'corridor' meetings of the type described here useful or not?
- Is the urgency portrayed to the student by the supervisor a wise move?

On collecting the three corrected chapters, Anthony was aghast to see the extent of the corrections Dr Good required. They involved modifying and moving sections of text from one chapter to another, almost totally re-referencing one of the chapters; updating the references in all three chapters; re-organization and re-tabulation of some of the data; expressing some of the tables as figures, in addition to what appeared to Anthony to be an inordinate number of typographical errors. In something of a panic, but also considerably irritated, Anthony returned home to look at the rest of his thesis write-up, and realized it was going to be a monumental task to re-organize this along the lines proposed by Dr Good, if she was going to demand a similar degree of change in the chapters she hadn't yet seen. The following day Anthony e-mailed Dr Good saying he couldn't possibly get the changes she required done in time, and also informed her he disagreed with quite a number of the changes she had suggested. He received a very brief e-mail response straightaway from Dr Good instructing him to come and see her immediately.

Points for Consideration

- To what extent is the supervisor responsible for the detailed write-up of a PhD thesis?
- Is the nature of the communication between supervisor and student acceptable in this scenario?
- How can this potential breakdown in the relationship between the student and the supervisor be prevented?
- Is the supervisor dealing with this matter realistically, given the tight deadlines?
- Is the student's response to the situation with which he is faced the most useful one in the circumstances?

The meeting between the student and the supervisor was somewhat confrontational. Dr Good took the line that the chapters she had seen were inexpertly set out with a good deal of sloppy text, much of the data had been under-interpreted or even wrongly interpreted in the light of recent references, some of the major points were not appropriately highlighted and, finally, the reference list was not sufficiently up-to-date. Dr Good added that although the data were excellent, she was damned if she was going to allow submission of a poor presentation, and possibly 'spoil the ship for a ha'porth of tar'! For his part, Anthony said Dr Good was being far too fussy and 'nit-picking', and he had 'lived' this work over the past three years. The main themes were very clearly set out in his opinion, and from what he'd seen of other students' theses from the department, including those from students under Dr Good's supervision, his presentation would stand on its merits and be acceptable to any External Examiner. In any case, Dr Good had said the data were excellent. Besides, his post-doctoral job in America was dependent on his being awarded his PhD before the end of the year. Further acrimonious discussion ensued before Anthony, inwardly raging, ended the meeting by stating that he would submit the thesis without Dr Good's blessing if necessary as he had a perfect right to! Dr Good's response to this tirade was simply to say that she thought this would be a most unwise course of action.

Points for Consideration

- Why has this meeting failed to resolve the situation?
- Who is at fault?
- Should the student allow his attitude to be influenced by his knowledge and appreciation of other PhD theses accessible to him?
- Should the student's future post-doctoral position influence his behaviour?
- Who bears the ultimate responsibility associated with the PhD write-up and submission?
- Why has the relationship between the student and the supervisor failed at this final hurdle?

These matters rested until four days before the submission deadline, when on returning from a conference, Dr Good found a complete, unbound thesis on her desk, with a note from Anthony to the effect that he had finished the write-up, had taken her comments into account, and would be grateful if she would 'run through' the thesis to check that it was OK before he submitted it on the following Tuesday.

Points for Consideration

- How might this situation have been avoided?
- Should a clearly excellent and confident student be left totally on his own to both write up and submit a PhD thesis?

Evolution of the problem

The unwritten 'contract' entered into by the student and the supervisor at the outset of a PhD research programme is that both will contribute to progressing the research work, and to production of the final written thesis. The student's decision to submit independently of the supervisor is effectively, a unilateral withdrawal from the 'contract', and will jeopardize the chances of a successful outcome to the PhD submission.

The last-minute loss of appropriate contact between the student and supervisor could possibly be due to assumptions by both parties, based on their previous successful relationship and knowledge of each other, that each was fully competent to complete the PhD process, and were fully aware of the tight deadlines involved.

There were no formal, regular meetings between student and supervisor to discuss the write-up at this crucial point in time for the thesis submission. 'Corridor' meetings are, of course, inappropriate and a sign of bad management.

The deadline imposed on the student by his being offered and accepting a post dependent on obtaining his PhD had increased the pressure on him, and by extension on the supervisor, which often leads to increased stress on both, which can result in a less than optimum handling of the situation.

The supervisor may not have requested much written work from the student earlier in the research programme. Most students will not be practised or experienced at thesis writing. Both supervisor and student were guilty of errors of judgement. The supervisor may well have overestimated the student's capabilities, particularly at writing, while the student underestimated the difficulty and time involved in the process of thesis write-up.

Possible prevention and resolution of the problem

1. The nature of the 'contract' between the student and supervisor regarding delivery of a successful PhD should be made clear to the former by the supervisor at the onset of the research work, namely that contributions and joint efforts from both of them throughout the duration of the research, in accordance with their respective roles, will optimize both the enjoyment of the experience and the chances of a successful outcome.
2. The supervisor should prepare the student for the thesis write-up stage by alerting him to the potential difficulties that may arise and the time that can be involved. It might be helpful if some form of written material, thesis chapters, conference papers for example, could be sought from the student in the second year or even earlier.
3. While it is only to be expected and, indeed, considered desirable that students will wish to progress their career prospects when opportunities

arise, supervisors should be aware that this may impose extra pressures on both the student and the supervisor, but particularly on the former. Supervisors should therefore exercise greater circumspection and tolerance in dealing with the student at this crucial time.

4. The supervisor should have had a greater knowledge of the student's capabilities. At the write-up stage regular contact with the student to assess progress would help the supervisor more readily gauge the student's writing abilities, although ideally this should be determined at an earlier stage.

5. It is the responsibility of the supervisor to resolve the current 'spat', and achieve the best outcome for the student, by meeting with the student, receiving and correcting the thesis chapters as rapidly as possible, while also ensuring that the student deals with these changes appropriately.

6. If the PhD *viva* examination date has not yet been agreed, the supervisor should discuss this with the Internal Examiner so that it can take place within the time-frames required, if at all possible. If this proves impossible, then the supervisor, with the approval of the student, may wish to contact the student's prospective employers in America to see if the student could take up the position one month later, for example.

24

An Issue of Priority

Scenario

Ivor Barlow, now reaching the end of his third year, had been an excellent PhD student and had been able to participate in, and contribute to, two potentially widely applicable advances in the research field of Child Education at Chesterbank University, where his supervisor was Professor Vince Easton. In fact, because of his research activities, Ivor had made something of a name for himself and had recently been offered a couple of posts, one of which he decided to accept. Even though the three-year period of his PhD registration was not quite up, his new employer, the local NHS Trust was keen for him to start his new job as soon as possible. Professor Easton had no problem with this, and was pleased that Ivor had been given such an excellent opportunity to develop his career. However, he did say to Ivor, that ideally, he would have much preferred it if Ivor could have completely written up his thesis before commencing his new job.

Point for Consideration

- With students experiencing financial problems in undergraduate years which will likely continue into postgraduate study, PhD students may wish to pay off debts as quickly as possible. This could lead to more students working while trying to write up their thesis.

By the time Ivor left the university to take up his new position, he was about one-third of the way through writing up his thesis, which Professor Easton considered a good start. As Ivor's PhD had been funded by the Economic and Social Research Council (ESRC), it was important for Professor Easton to ensure that his student's PhD was submitted before the four-year time limit, or financial penalties could be imposed. Professor Easton therefore suggested that Ivor should keep in touch with him by e-mail on a regular basis, that they would meet in person whenever possible, and that Ivor should send him those sections or chapters of his thesis as he completed the writing of them, in order that Professor Easton could correct them as required. Ivor was very pleased at this suggestion and also very keen to finish and submit his thesis, and be awarded his PhD. What Ivor had not anticipated, however, were the demands that his new position would make on him, and although his new job was very interesting and exciting, it was also extremely time-consuming.

Points for Consideration

- Is it possible that pressures to write up and complete the PhD for reasons of funding, supervisor availability and RAE ratings may influence the quality of the PhD thesis or the research produced?
- What is the rationale of the PhD for the student?
- For the supervisor?

After a couple of months and several exchanges by e-mail, Ivor managed to find the time to meet Professor Easton. Ivor was pleased to see him again and keen to discuss the progress and problems he was experiencing in his employment. At the same time, however, he was apologetic for his lack of progress with the write-up of his thesis, but informed Professor Easton that now he had settled into his job, he would definitely be able to find the time to move this along. Professor Easton, for his part, said he understood Ivor's situation, and reassured Ivor that as long as he now went 'hard at it', he felt sure he still had time to complete within four years. About a week later, Ivor's current line manager was taken seriously ill and Ivor was asked to cover for her in her absence. In some ways this was a great opportunity for Ivor and he was eager to face this new challenge and also pleased about the temporary rise in salary that was entailed.

Point for Consideration

- What would you consider to be the priorities under these circumstances, completion of the write-up and PhD submission or the launching of the student's career?

The problem for Ivor, of course, was that he now had even less time of his own to work on his thesis, and to be honest, at the end of a strenuous day's work, he did not really feel like working any more, especially on something as demanding as his thesis write-up. After another couple of months, Professor Easton became anxious to meet with Ivor again to review his progress, although he had not received any chapters or work from Ivor in the intervening time period. Ivor, however, was still incredibly busy at work and had little chance to take time out for an additional meeting. Moreover, he was starting to feel guilty about his lack of progress and did not really relish the thought of what might well turn out to be a difficult confrontation with Professor Easton. When Ivor responded to Professor Easton, saying that a meeting just wasn't possible at the moment, the latter became somewhat concerned. He had received no work from Ivor on his thesis since he had started his job, and really for the first time, began to consider the possibility that the student's four-year write-up target might not be met.

In due course, the four-year write-up target came around, and Professor Easton had still not succeeded in organizing a meeting with Ivor, although he had, in fact, met Ivor unexpectedly at a conference but there had been little time to discuss the thesis. Ivor had been relieved at this as he was well aware that the progress on his write-up could at best, be only called minimal. Initially, Ivor had felt guilty at not having worked on his thesis but now could not face thinking about it, especially as he was doing well at his job, and his employers seemed to think that lack of a PhD degree would not prove any hindrance to his career prospects in his current employment.

Professor Eaton was both annoyed and disappointed at this outcome. He had really believed that a student of Ivor's calibre would have been able to complete his thesis on time despite the fact that he had a job. He felt frustrated and at a loss as to what he could do. He knew that both the Research Council and the university would be unhappy and concerned about Ivor's situation, but he realized it was becoming increasingly difficult for him to persuade or cajole Ivor into completing his write-up, submitting his thesis and gaining his well-earned PhD.

Points for Consideration

- What incentives or motivating influences are available to a supervisor to get a student, in these circumstances, to complete the write-up?
- What factors, other than personal satisfaction, make it most important and advisable for a student to fulfil his PhD work, and gain the award?

Evolution of the problem

The failure of both supervisor or student to effectively prioritize the thesis write-up in the unfolding circumstances of the employment prospects of the student is the primary cause of this well-recognized problem.

When a student has left the university, it is easy to let time slip by despite good intentions, and when the student's employment carries no incentives to complete write-up, submit and be awarded the PhD degree, the longer this situation continues, the less likely it is that the student will ever complete the degree.

In effect, once the student had started in his new post, any influence the supervisor might have had will be greatly reduced. Occasional meetings and contact by e-mail is the best the supervisor could aim for, as the principal day-to-day responsibility of his former student is now bound to be his employers.

Although a supervisor may be aware of difficulties that can arise with respect to students who have not completed their write-up before taking up full-time career employment, the obvious capabilities, research competence and motivation of the student in this case seem to have, unwisely, allayed the concerns of his supervisor.

When a student puts off and fails to meet a supervisor over a period of time and keeps making excuses, it often indicates that the student is having difficulties with the write-up. Failure of the student to meet with the supervisor and his avoidance of contact with him merely exacerbate the problem further.

Possible prevention and resolution of the problem

1. It is almost invariably in the best interests of the student that the write-up of a thesis be completed before the student leaves the university environment, and this should be clearly acknowledged and indicated to the student by the supervisor as a major priority. A successfully completed and awarded PhD degree will usually be of benefit to the student in progressing the early stages of their career.
2. It is important to stress to students that trying to write up while holding down a full-time job can be extremely difficult for a variety of reasons. If, however, this has to happen, then serious planning for the write-up needs to take place between supervisor and student. Ideally, a suitable but strict timetable should be recommended.
3. It is essential that the supervisor and student keep in touch on a regular basis and with e-mail this should be relatively easy; meetings may be more of a problem but it is vital to maintain contact. Even if progress on the thesis is slow in the early stages of working, at least the momentum has been maintained. The responsibility for making progress on the write-up rests with the supervisor.
4. Additional pressure and encouragement can be applied to the student by the departmental Graduate Tutor and/or the Head of Department. However, the student ultimately has to make the personal effort to complete the work, and the university can only try to bring the matter to a satisfactory conclusion.

25

An Issue of Write-Up

Scenario

Antoinette's research work on the potential impact of asylum seekers on small, rural village communities in Yorkshire had progressed slowly. Admittedly, she had had several problems, including difficulties in both reading and writing English, even though she had met requirements for entry to the department's PhD programme, while a motor accident to her father had necessitated her returning home to North Africa for six weeks towards the end of her second year. But now, early in June of her third year, she could start writing up, as all her questionnaires were back, and her interviews completed.

Points for Consideration

- When should the write-up of the PhD be started?
- How is it decided that the student has enough quality work for use in the thesis write-up?

However, the data she had accumulated gave Antoinette considerable worry. How best should she arrange them? Which was sound data and which might be problematic? Had she covered all the possible angles on the work? Would the examiners pick holes in, and find fault with, the approaches she had used? How should she interpret some of her more complex findings where evidence in the recent literature showed diverse and contentious viewpoints on one of her major findings? She appreciated that the subtle and closely argued nuances she would be required to express in order to provide an accurate, yet clear and focused interpretation of her data would not be easy for her in what was, in effect, a foreign language.

> **Points for Consideration**
>
> • What are the mechanics of constructing the PhD thesis?
> • How should the student be instructed with regard to commencing the write-up?
> • How should specific problems such as contentious issues be dealt with in the write-up?

Four weeks later, having managed to organize the results and attempt the discussion for two chapters, Antoinette received an e-mail from her supervisor requesting a meeting the following week to run through her draft write-up and finalize the submission date for her thesis. Antoinette panicked and decided to re-write the work she'd already done, but two days before the meeting, the revised version seemed to Antoinette to be even more muddled, and she e-mailed Dr Newby, her supervisor, asking to postpone the meeting for a week.

> **Points for Consideration**
>
> • Has the supervisor assumed too much here?
> • What does the student's reaction say about her state of mind and her character?

At 30 years of age, Dr Newby was three years into his first academic post, and Antoinette was his first PhD student. Although the main supervisor, Dr Newby was jointly supervising Antoinette with a senior, experienced colleague. On receiving Antoinette's e-mail, he had readily agreed to put the meeting off as he had found Antoinette a difficult and somewhat unresponsive student, far less motivated and perceptive than his second-year PhD student, who had already given him, unsolicited, one draft thesis chapter. He felt quite relieved as he would not now have to think about Antoinette's write-up during his summer break. He replied that he would contact her on his return from his trip to California.

> **Points for Consideration**
>
> • Should the supervisor have agreed to the postponement of the meeting?
> • Is the supervisor's graduate student allocation an appropriate one for a young member of the academic staff?
> • What do you think of the supervisor's perceptions of his two PhD students?
> • How much time should be allowed for the thesis write-up?

It was in the last week of August that Antoinette received an e-mail from her supervisor proposing a meeting two weeks later. Dr Newby's message indicated that he anticipated Antoinette would have completed most of her draft write-up, and that he could check through it. Through the summer Antoinette had worried about her write-up, and whenever she looked at the computer screen, making sense of the complicated array of information, and expressing it clearly and concisely in English seemed impossible. Her supervisor's e-mail threw her into a further panic, and she requested a delay of the meeting while she 'tidied things up'.

Points for Consideration

- Is the supervisor expecting too much of the student?
- Is there an optimum way of managing the write-up for this student?
- Is there any source, other than the main supervisor, where the student can obtain help?
- What are the pressures on a supervisor at this stage of a PhD research programme?

Meanwhile, a phone call from Antoinette's second supervisor alerted Dr Newby that time was running short, and a meeting between Antoinette and both supervisors was hastily arranged. At the meeting it was clear to the supervisors that although there was almost a complete draft thesis, both the writing and the organization of the work left much to be desired, and also, due to the somewhat ambiguous nature of some of the data, very precise interpretations and carefully worded summations of the work were required.

Points for Consideration

- When, if at all, should the second supervisor have become involved in this situation?
- Who should have been pro-active in involving the second supervisor?
- Why might the second supervisor not have been involved?
- How may the problems of the draft thesis be resolved?

In view of the time constraints on PhD submissions imposed by both the university and Dr Newby's department, twice-weekly meetings between Antoinette and her supervisor were arranged to deal with the thesis, and a mock *viva* examination with both supervisors was set up for Antoinette.

Points for Consideration

- Are these arrangements sufficient to resolve Antoinette's difficulties?
- Are mock *viva* examinations a good idea?

The topic of the *viva* examiners was also discussed at the meeting, and the decision was made to ask Professor Michael Holmes from the Oxton University Department of Social and Psychological Health to act as the External Examiner. Dr Jim Gold was thought appropriate for the Internal Examiner. Although she made no comment, Antoinette was somewhat disturbed that Professor Holmes was to be approached to be her External. Other students had talked about him, and his reputation as a pernickety stickler for accuracy, and his entrenched position relating to at least one of Antoinette's areas of research made her almost quake in her shoes.

Points for Consideration

- How should the choice of examiners for a PhD thesis be made?
- Is it important to take the student's views into account?
- Should the student make her views known, and if so, how?

Evolution of the problem

There appeared to be too much data, too many interweaving factors for the relatively inexperienced graduate student, lacking the more extensive background knowledge of the experienced supervisor, to marshal and deal with.

There was no guidance on the write-up provided by the supervisor. The supervisor seemed to be sending out the wrong signals regarding the difficulty which the write-up entails, perhaps due to prior, limited, experience, and showing a lack of insight into the situation.

An overseas graduate student with English as the second language, might not have the necessary skills to assess the nuances and subtleties required to successfully interpret a complex set of results and weave them into the background of the topic in the required discussions.

There was procrastination by both the student (understandable under the circumstances), and the supervisor (unforgivable).

There was a lack of sufficient or appropriate discussion with the student *vis-à-vis* the selection of examiners.

Possible prevention and resolution of the problem

1. The student should be asked to analyse, interpret and organize data as the PhD programme progresses, and to write up some results, either for presentation for 'in-house' reports, or for publication, if appropriate.
2. Some guidance and information on thesis writing and preparation should be made available to the student earlier in the research programme. At

the very least, meetings discussing the write-up in some detail should take place between the supervisor and the student early in the final year, or in some subjects at an even earlier stage.

3. There should have been involvement of the more experienced co-supervisor earlier, ideally when any problem of this nature is first recognized, and when the main supervisor starts to feel uneasy (or guilty) about the situation.

4. Both student and supervisor will need to 'burn the midnight oil' to bring the thesis to a successful outcome in the relatively short time officially available to them.

5. The views of the student on the selection of the examiners for the PhD thesis should be sought and receive careful consideration.

6. The working relationship between the supervisor and the student should ideally be one of informality and mutual respect relatively early in the research programme. Such a relationship would hopefully avoid any procrastination, especially on the part of the graduate student, when, and if, the timelines get short towards the end of the research programme. The student should feel comfortable approaching the supervisor with any real or perceived problems over the duration of their working relationship. (It should, however, be recognized that the above working relationship may not always be the most appropriate one.)

26

An Issue of *Viva* Preparation

Scenario

Aled could not honestly say he had enjoyed his three years in the Department of Asian Studies at the University of Norfolk investigating ancient texts of Southeast Asia and the influence they had exerted on modern religious thought in the region. He was particularly nervous about, and dreading, his *viva* examination that was now fast approaching. Aled had a quiet, unassuming, introspective personality, and appeared to his supervisor, even after three years, to be difficult to deal with, although his research studies had progressed smoothly enough.

Points for Consideration

- What is the importance of a graduate student's interpersonal skills to a supervisor?
- To what extent should such skills determine graduate student selection?
- Should graduate student selection be based solely on perceived research potential?

Dr Warris, his supervisor, although aware from the almost finished thesis write-up, that Aled was fully versant with the area of knowledge immediately surrounding his studies, felt that there might be problems for Aled at his *viva* examination on two counts. First, he was not sure Aled had undertaken sufficient breadth of reading to put his work into the larger perspective; more worryingly though, Aled was not naturally talkative, seemed to have difficulties in explaining the subtleties and nuances abounding in the thesis write-up of his research studies, and needed considerable prompting to come forth with a train of thought that would demonstrate his undoubted intellectual capacity, or to speculate on the possible implications of his conclusions. He even seemed to find it awkward to describe clearly the relevance and relative merits of the source material that formed the basis of his investigations. With both his peers and the academic staff in the department, he always seemed ill-at-ease and diffident, communicating, even in relaxed social conditions, only with difficulty, and was clearly poor at thinking on his feet.

Point for Consideration

- What Research Training Programme (RTP) modules might this student usefully have attended?

Reflecting on the past three years, Dr Warris recalled that he had been desperate to find a student, partly to complete an unfinished study, but also because his own CV needed bolstering. From the outset, Aled had been unforthcoming, reserved, shy and nervous, but his diligence, his clear enthusiasm for 'grubbing around in arcane and disputed texts', solitary sort of work, together with his upbringing in Southeast Asia and his apparent determination to follow a career studying the early and primitive texts of the region, had overridden any doubts that Dr Warris had harboured about his interpersonal skills. Now, however, although Aled's thesis appeared very competently put together, his verbal communication difficulties had not improved, and Dr Warris was at a loss to see any way whereby he could avoid a *viva* examination travesty, in which Aled's contribution might prove to be woefully inadequate, fail to reveal his true capabilities as a research worker to the examiners and set up an uncomfortable mis-match between the thesis presentation and the *viva* performance.

Points for Consideration

- What is the relative importance of the written thesis compared to the *viva* performance of a graduate student, in determining the award of a PhD degree?
- In what way might poor interpersonal skills prove a barrier to career progression?
- Should the importance of career progression for a supervisor be a major factor in accepting a graduate research student?

Nevertheless, Dr Warris was convinced it would be difficult for Aled to fail his PhD, even if the *viva* examination proved disastrous, but Aled's performance could be an influence on his future career in the field, particularly as his External Examiner was a senior staff member of the most prestigious academic Department of Asian Studies in the country. A poor performance could also reflect badly on Dr Warris himself, on his department and on the university.

Aled had given talks about his studies, as required by the department, in each of the first two years of his PhD. Both had been stuttering, unconvincing and even embarrassing presentations. He had coped badly with the questions he had received and had appeared highly agitated at the end of each of the talks.

Points for Consideration

- What are the aims of graduate student talks and presentations?
- Who should identify and address student problems of communication and interpersonal skills?
- At what point during the PhD programme should these problems be addressed?
- What are the merits of an internal, *viva* type of interview examination at the time of transfer at the end of the first year?

Because of these problems, and the lack of any improvement in them, Dr Warris decided that in the two months leading up to the *viva* examination, he would have to provide Aled with all the extra support and encouragement he could muster at this late stage. Prior to Aled's final year presentation, which was due shortly, he would prime him with one or more preliminary deliveries of his talk in his, Dr Warris's, presence alone; he would alert Aled's Internal Examiner, who knew something of Aled's problems, that the *viva* examination could well be very hard work, involving a great deal of cajoling, perhaps some 'shock tactics' and a considerable amount of patience and probing to achieve any headway.

Points for Consideration

- On what basis are Internal Examiners selected?
- Can they play a role in the lead-up to the *viva* examination?

After two trial runs of Aled's final year presentation to Dr Warris, and a lengthy talk between them concerning his nervousness and diffidence, Aled seemed slightly more confident, and although neither of the deliveries had shown huge improvements, Dr Warris thought he saw a glimmer of hope. Aled was well aware of his problems, but said he always 'went to pieces' when faced with speaking to his peers, and particularly senior staff, in a formal setting. In spite of this, Aled's final year presentation proved only marginally better than his earlier ones; he lost the thread of his talk on one occasion, spoke in a clearly nervous, mumbling manner and appeared not to understand, responding confusingly to relatively straightforward questions.

The last resort of support available for Aled was a 'mock *viva*', but Dr Warris felt this was a 'double-edged sword'. Even if he found a colleague willing to give up the time required, how should Aled be handled in the mock *viva* situation? The aim would be to bolster Aled's confidence by familiarizing him with the *viva* situation, and give him time to marshal his thoughts, and state them as lucidly and naturally as possible, while under some pressure. The mock *viva* might also allow the mock examiners to identify, and stress for Aled, specific points in the thesis that he might be asked to defend. All this had to be achieved in a manner that would not reduce or destroy what little confidence Aled might already have. Not a task that Dr Warris relished! Nevertheless, having approached Aled to ascertain his willingness for the mock *viva* to take place, having found a suitable room, having found and briefed a colleague prepared to take part, and having devised lines of questioning that might set Aled at some ease and get him talking, Dr Warris duly arranged the mock *viva* examination a week prior to the real *viva* examination.

Points for Consideration

- Is a mock *viva* a good idea for this particular student?
- How could the time being spent by the supervisor on this student at this stage be avoided?
- Are other means available to help the student at this point in time?
- Is the idea of some form of training in dealing with the approach to a *viva* examination, a valid one?
- If so, at what point should it be available?

Although at the outset, when assisted by some gentle cajoling and good-natured probing on the part of the 'examiners', all went well, and Aled showed signs he could cope with unintimidating, non-aggressive, gentle, amiable and relatively simple questioning, a particular, less benevolent, sharper and more complex query from Dr Warris's colleague, seemed to make Aled very uncomfortable. He became visibly nervous, faltered over his words, appeared 'thrown' by the question and appeared unable to grasp its point. Subsequently, even when the question was rephrased and delivered in a less inimical, and more clearly delineated way, Aled was unable to provide any satisfactory, well-expressed and pertinent response. From that point on, and despite Dr Warris's best efforts, Aled's performance deteriorated almost to the point of embarrassment, and the examiners abandoned the mock *viva* after only 40 minutes.

Points for Consideration

- Given that a mock *viva* is an acceptable tool for student support, to what extent should it be planned?
- Can a student be fully examined in a *viva* examination without some in-depth criticism and 'aggressive' probing of their work?

In a subsequent talk, Aled appeared very distressed, and it was apparent to Dr Warris that the mock *viva* examination had not succeeded in allaying Aled's, or indeed, his own concerns, and might even have made matters worse. Despite a further attempt at a confidence-boosting pep-talk, it appeared to the supervisor that short of arranging for Aled to have urgent hypnotism or psychotherapy, there was nothing more he could do. Aled would have to face the Examiners in his current, discomposed state. His performance in the *viva* examination, and its outcome, would be in the lap of the gods.

Points for Consideration

- Is it appropriate to alert the Examiners to the student's current state?
- Would it be possible, or advisable, to postpone the *viva* examination on medical grounds?

Evolution of the problem

The rationale for selection of a student for a PhD research programme should primarily be based on perceived research potential, appropriate academic background, commitment and enthusiasm. Personality deficiencies such as poor communication or interpersonal skills in a student will make the establishment of a student–supervisor relationship, and consequently clear progress of the research work, considerably more difficult for the supervisor.

A supervisor should not consider accepting a student onto a PhD research programme for reasons that are primarily concerned with his own career progression. Students selected for reasons other than those indicated above will often create problems for the supervisor, the department and sometimes the institution during their research studies or examination.

The student did not attend, either of his own volition or on the recommendation of the supervisor or department, any RTP modules that might have been of benefit to him and might have improved his communication and interpersonal skills.

Although the problems of the student were recognized at selection and the start of the research programme, they were either not considered important enough to be addressed, or else were completely overlooked even after poor presentations in both year one and year two. The thesis is the major element of the PhD examination, providing evidence of the student's research methodology, research strategy, written, organizational and presentational skills. Examiners would expect a competent thesis to be supported and defended by a student at the *viva* examination stage in a confident manner that clearly shows the student's intellectual ability, understanding and knowledge of research methodology, data interpretational skills and mental agility. Poor communication and interpersonal skills will hamper the student in demonstrating his research competence, and, if not overcome, can act as an impediment to a career in research.

The student's communication and interpersonal problems were not picked up at the transfer stage, due either to the nature of the transfer process in the department (no *viva*-type interview) or else they were considered unimportant or irrelevant in view of the excellence of the student's research.

Due to the failure to deal with the student's problems earlier, both supervisor and student are now having to devote considerable time in a damage-limitation exercise.

No formal or informal talks, seminars, question and answer sessions, other forms of information were provided by the institution, and available to the student, to prepare, raise the awareness of, and deal with student concerns about the lead-up to, and form of the *viva* examination.

The mock *viva* examination appeared to have been unhelpful in this instance, perhaps because it was undertaken too close in time to the real examination. The supervisors' arrangements to help the student in the period leading up to the *viva* examination came too late to address the student's problems. However, it may be that the student's personality problems and deficiencies were intractable. If so, it is arguable that anything would have been of help at this stage, for this student.

Possible prevention and resolution of the problem

1. Although selection of the student for a PhD research programme was made on correct grounds, the student's problems should be highlighted at this stage, discussed by the supervisor with colleagues, and courses and RTP modules of benefit to the student identified.
2. The supervisor should be under no pressure to accept a student he considers unsuitable for a PhD research programme under his guidance and supervision. However, the supervisor should consider the academic background, perceived research potential and capabilities of a prospective student against any real or perceived shortcomings in the student and make a balanced decision.
3. The student must be directed to attend any RTP modules most suited to his needs.

4. The supervisor, with the help of the Graduate Tutor or experienced colleagues, should assist the student through informal (perhaps on a one-to-one basis) or formal presentations and advice, to improve his communication and interpersonal skills through his first and second years. This may include preparing the student for his transfer, and requesting that the transfer panel give the student a mock *viva* interview, if this does not already form part of the transfer process. In most cases, such a programme will improve or alleviate the student's problems, and avoid a last-minute panic and possible deterioration of the student's performance.

5. Talks, seminars or question and answer sessions should be made available by the university on both thesis writing and preparation for the *viva* examination for students in the final year of their PhD research programme.

6. Internal Examiners are selected to ensure fair play in the conduct of the examination, on the basis of their appositeness for examining the student's research, and to provide a liaison between the department, the institution, the student's supervisor and the External Examiner. As such, they may be approached by the supervisor to highlight any problems, such as excessive student nervousness, that, in the judgement of the Internal Examiner, may be passed on to the External Examiner, either prior to, or at the time of, the *viva* examination.

7. To gain a PhD, the student has to fulfil the requirements of the university, and for most this involves a *viva* examination. Unless the student becomes physically ill, the examination should not be postponed. It may, however, be deemed appropriate to suggest that the student seek some counselling or medical help at sometime during the PhD programme, if only to ascertain the likelihood of any improvement of the problem.

27

An Issue of Identity

Jackie Marsh

Scenario

Sabi had applied to her local university to undertake a part-time PhD. She wanted to study the experiences of gay and lesbian parents as they dealt with their children's schools. Sabi did not know any of the staff in the department, and therefore had not identified a specific person that she would like to act as her supervisor.

The Head of the Research Degrees Programme received Sabi's application form and proposal. If an applicant had not specified a particular supervisor, the proposal was passed on for consideration to staff she felt might be interested in supervising in that particular area of research. She felt unsure in Sabi's case. There was a gay lecturer in the Department, Dr Iqbal – would he be the most suitable supervisor for this student? However, his research focused on gay male teachers, whereas another lecturer, Dr Ann Bates, was an expert on home–school relations.

Point for Consideration

- How far should a Research Degrees Co-ordinator or Selector liaise with a student about potential supervisors?

The Head of Research Degrees decided to pass the proposal onto the lecturer who had experience in researching home–school relations, Dr Bates, for consideration. Dr Bates felt that this would be an interesting study to supervise and therefore set up the first meeting with Sabi. At the meeting, Sabi explained that her interest in this topic arose from her own experiences of being a lesbian parent who had had a difficult relationship with her son's primary school.

Dr Bates suggested that Sabi should not let her own experiences cloud her judgement about the topic; she should keep an open mind in order to ensure that she remained objective.

Points for Consideration

- Can the research process ever be objective?
- If someone has a strong personal investment in a particular issue, would that present problems in carrying out research in that area?

The first part of the research process went very well. Dr Bates was very familiar with relevant literature relating to home–school relationships and gave Sabi much support in weaving her way through this complex field.

Sabi began preparing for the fieldwork, which would involve conducting semi-structured interviews with 20 gay and lesbian parents. She decided to recruit research participants through a national organization for gay and lesbian parents. Dr Bates gave Sabi advice on the wording of the letters to parents in this organization. However, Sabi did not state in the letter that she was a lesbian parent herself and asked Dr Bates if she should include this information. Dr Bates told Sabi that she did not consider this to be an important factor for consideration, the main point of the letter was to outline what the research process would involve.

Points for Consideration

- When recruiting participants for a research project which focuses on issues relating to their identity in terms of 'race', ethnicity, sexuality, physical ability or other aspects of identity, how important is it for students to identify their own positionality to participants?
- Was the behaviour of Dr Bates ethical in this instance?
- Did her advice correspond to guidance given in the British Educational Research Association's (BERA) *Revised Ethical Guidance for Educational Research* (2004)?

Eventually, Sabi managed to recruit the parents she required for her interviews. She had spent some weeks developing a detailed interview schedule. However, Sabi was rather upset when she received some feedback from Dr Bates on the interview questions. Dr Bates felt that some of the questions were not relevant to the study because they asked about issues such as whether or not respondents had suffered from homophobia themselves as school pupils. Dr Bates suggested that Sabi should focus on the main issue, the relationship they had with their children's schools. For her part, Sabi felt that these types of questions were important, as such experiences could affect how the parents felt towards schools and therefore could impact on their abilities to build good relationships with their children's schools.

Points for Consideration

- Should the supervisor raise concerns about the interview questions at this stage?
- Would reflection on the outcomes of piloting the interview questions first help?

However, keen to receive the approval of her supervisor, Sabi removed the disputed questions, but she felt quite cross and frustrated about it. She would have liked to have talked to someone else in the department about the increasing frustration with some of Dr Bates's views, but was not sure if she was able to do this.

Sabi developed quite complex primary and secondary codes for the data. However, she became disappointed during one meeting with her supervisor, when Dr Bates challenged her interpretation of the data. Sabi had felt that a recurrent experience of many of the parents related to the lack of literature from school, which they felt recognized their family situations.

Point for Consideration

- What should be the procedure if a supervisor wishes to challenge a student's interpretation of data?

For example, school prospectuses always had pictures of mothers and fathers at parents' evening together. Sabi identified this as an instance of homophobia on the part of the school. Dr Bates, however, suggested that experience from her own research would suggest that literature from school always excluded some families, whether gay or heterosexual – what about the lack of translated material for bilingual families, for example? This was, therefore, not a key issue that Sabi should focus on, especially given the wealth of other data she had. Sabi did not feel confident enough to counter Dr Bates's argument, but she felt very reluctant to draw back from identifying this as an important aspect of her data. Sabi was beginning to think that Dr Bates's lack of understanding of gay and lesbian issues was affecting the nature of the supervision, as Sabi was feeling reluctant to raise what she felt were important issues, in case Dr Bates felt she was exaggerating them, or considered her to have 'a chip on her shoulder'. Nevertheless, Sabi continued to make progress and successfully completed the transfer procedure.

Point for Consideration

- What support should a department offer students who feel that their supervisors' own misunderstanding of key issues is affecting their progress?

Despite Sabi's reservations, she continued to work with Dr Bates, who provided very helpful feedback on the structure of the final thesis, despite the differences in opinion over aspects of the data. Sabi expected to complete the thesis in a few months, and so it was time to think about who should be appointed as examiners. Dr Bates did consult with students on this matter, although she always had the final decision. Both Sabi and Dr Bates felt that Dr Sanders would be a suitable Internal Examiner, as his research focused on home–school relations. He had worked alongside Dr Bates on a number of research projects and was highly respected within the department as a fair and rigorous examiner.

Points for Consideration

- How much involvement should a student have in choosing examiners?
- In situations such as this, where a student has conducted research on issues relating to discrimination, marginalization and oppression, how important is it to have an examiner who understands these issues in general, rather than in the specific context in which the research took place?

However, there was lack of agreement about the External Examiner. Sabi suggested an academic, Professor Ryan, whom she knew had experience of conducting extensive interviews with gay and lesbian research participants on a range of issues which involved a focus on discrimination. As a lesbian, Professor Ryan had also written about methodological issues relating to identity and positionality. However, Professor Ryan was a sociologist and had never conducted research within an educational context. Dr Bates's view was that it would be more appropriate to ask an External Examiner she knew, and whose research had been based in schools, Professor Szczerba and, indeed, Sabi had cited his work extensively in the thesis. She suggested to Sabi that Sabi's work would have more credibility within the educational field if she had an External Examiner whose work was respected in this area. Sabi agreed with Dr Bates's choices as she felt she knew best, given her knowledge of the educational field, and the External Examiner recommended by Dr Bates was accordingly appointed.

The *viva* went very well and Sabi was informed that she had been recommended for the award of a PhD, subject to some minor amendments. Feeling elated, Sabi left the examination room only to feel thoroughly deflated when Dr Bates remarked how relieved she had been everything went so well, given the concerns she herself had had about Sabi's overemphasis on the homophobia of schools at the expense of other issues, such as the structural barriers which affected home–school relationships.

> **Point for Consideration**
>
> • Should a supervisor tell a student about concerns (however valid) they have about a thesis after the *viva*?

Evolution of the problem

There was no liaison with the student about the choice of supervisor to begin with.

The supervisor imposed her own views on the student's work too frequently, instead of taking on board the student's views about identity and data analysis. The difficulties lay in the supervisor's lack of understanding about some of the substantive issues that the student was researching. This supervisor had not sufficiently considered issues relating to homophobia and needed further awareness training.

The supervisor should have taken on board the student's feelings about the External Examiner.

The remark made by the supervisor after the *viva* was unprofessional and inappropriate. Homophobia was a key issue that the student had focused upon and it was therefore appropriate to emphasize this, both in the thesis and in the *viva* examination.

Possible prevention and resolution of the problem

1. Students should be involved in discussions about potential supervisors where possible. In cases where students are examining a topic which deals with issues of discrimination and oppression, then the involvement of a supervisor who has experience of research relating to these issues is valuable. If this is not possible, then an institution should be confident that other potential supervisors will understand the issues sufficiently to support the student's progress. In this case, Dr Iqbal could have been asked to be the second supervisor.

2. Students should be allocated a supervisor who is sympathetic to the student's epistemological and methodological concerns. In this case, the student's own identity and life experiences were central to the study and she should have been advised to reflect on this in the thesis.

3. If a supervisor does not have sufficient understanding of issues relating to a particular area, in this case, gay and lesbian studies, then he or she should seek advice from appropriate sources. For example, in this case study, the supervisor could have sought advice about the wording of letters to be sent out to potential research participants. Potential participants may

have found it useful to know about the researcher's own sexuality and experiences as a lesbian mother, as some may have been more willing to disclose their own experiences to someone who had undergone similar discriminatory practices.

4. Student's views on the selection of examiners should be sought and should receive careful consideration.
5. Any concerns a supervisor has about a thesis should be raised with a student before the *viva* examination.
6. Students should be given clear guidance on the procedures for reporting difficulties with tutors. In cases which involve some form of discrimination, e.g. racism, sexism, homophobia, then departments should adhere to the particular university's equal opportunities policy. Staff and students should be made aware of these policies and staff should be offered additional awareness training if required.

28

An Issue of Alleged Fraud

Scenario

Dr Porteous had agreed to accept Adrian as his research student even though the proposed project was not exactly in his own area of research work, as there was no more appropriate supervisor available in the department. However, after a relatively straightforward three years of research, things seemed to have turned out well, but Dr Porteous was nevertheless delighted that the door had finally closed behind Adrian as he entered his *viva voce* examination. Although there had been one or two difficult periods over the three years, Adrian's studies concerning the introduction of Christianity into areas on the Essex coastline, as evidenced by field archaeological investigations, had proved intriguing, productive and most worthwhile. After an unrewarding first 18 months work with no finds of relevance for the study, and little information from the most appropriate layers in the excavation, Dr Porteous had returned to his department at the University of Ipsworth from a two months combined vacation and dig in the Mediterranean, to find Adrian had unearthed three fragments of what seemed, from the lettering and figure carvings on them, to be a sixth- or seventh-century religious panel.

Points for Consideration

- How relevant, in terms of research interests, should the supervisor be with regards to the proposed research project?
- Should a 'deputy' supervisor be available when a supervisor is on prolonged absence?
- Should there be dual supervision as a matter of course?
- How closely should a student be supervised on a day-to-day basis?

Because of the unusual and unexpected nature of these finds, Dr Porteous had requested Adrian to take the fragments to the Museum of Essex Antiquities in Ipsworth where their date and authenticity were verified over the next six months. After much more archive work, involving both Adrian and Dr Porteous, the possible origin of the finds was identified as being a region east of Milan in northern Italy, where there was a known Christian site. Hitherto, there had been one or two finds indicating the possibility, but no more, of a link between early Christianity in Essex and northwest Italy. Adrian's finds had caused considerable local interest and became the lynchpin of his research work and thesis.

Points for Consideration

- Would you think that the circumstances under which the finds were made would arouse any suspicions?
- Did the supervisor act correctly in not questioning more thoroughly the circumstances surrounding the finds?

Adrian's *viva* had been in progress for about one-and-a-half hours, when his examiners appeared in Dr Porteous's office, in a state of some agitation. 'We've had a problem with Adrian's fieldwork and thesis,' said the External Examiner. 'We believe he may have been cheating and has possibly perpetrated a fraud with regard to the artefacts he's claiming he found at the dig. We need to discuss all aspects of this with you straightaway. The candidate is in the Head of Department's office in a bit of a state.'

Points for Consideration

- Has the 'discovery' of the alleged fraud been conducted in the most appropriate manner?
- Given that the matter has been suddenly and unexpectedly revealed, when is the best time to start resolving the situation?
- When might the External Examiner have voiced his suspicions concerning the work?
- With whom might he have discussed his concerns?
- Could he have requested more information during his reading of the thesis?
- Is it fair to the student, and indeed to all concerned, to open up these matters at the *viva* examination?

After the initial shock had subsided, Dr Porteous and the examiners began a detailed discussion concerning the exposure of the alleged fraud, and the manner in which Adrian had discovered the three, now disputed, fragments.

As the discussion progressed, it was revealed, through phone calls to other departmental staff, that while Dr Porteous had been away in the summer, Adrian had been working alone and unsupervised in the main trench on a number of occasions, and it was during one of these periods that the new finds had been made. Dr Porteous then recalled that one of his post-doctoral colleagues at the dig had informed him that one morning Adrian had called him over to look at two of the fragments in question, which Adrian had found while working late and alone the preceding evening. Together, as they had carefully exposed the fragments, Adrian had drawn his attention to a further piece of what looked like the same material partially exposed in the same layer, nearby. He and Adrian had dug this out, and taken all three finds to the on-site laboratory tent for examination and cleaning. These were immediately seized upon by the senior scientist on site at the time, who had recognized their probable importance, but had also severely remonstrated with both Adrian and the post-doctoral worker, for not leaving the fragments *in situ* for inspection, prior to their removal.

As the discussions continued, the External Examiner informed Dr Porteous that what had initially alerted him to the possibility that there might have been some duplicity, were discrepancies in Adrian's description, during the *viva* examination, of the discovery of the fragments compared to what he had written in the thesis. More damning, however, was the External Examiner's recollection of a small group of artefacts, supposedly originating from the same area in Italy, that had been reported at a conference about 25 years earlier. The External Examiner's memory of these objects was due to work he had been undertaking in the region at the time, and his discussions at that conference had raised doubts in his mind about the provenance of the artefacts. Subsequently, he had tried to contact the authors of the abstract to examine the artefacts in question, but had been unsuccessful. He had then moved on to work in other archaeological areas and the matter had passed from his mind.

Points for Consideration

- Who is at fault in the series of events that culminated in the acceptance of the finds as genuine and why?
- Should anyone else be involved in these discussions at this point?
- When should the university authorities be informed?

While reading Adrian's thesis, the External Examiner said he had recalled these matters, and during the *viva* examination had asked Adrian about the possible existence of other artefacts from the area without revealing his own memories and knowledge. To his surprise, Adrian had suggested that there might be similar finds waiting to be made, but on further questioning about why this might be so, had become embarrassed, failed to produce a logical reason, and blustered some response to the effect that he had spoken to other researchers at meetings who had suggested he should look elsewhere for similar objects in the region. After further questioning Adrian revealed that, although he did not know which site they had come from, there were what he thought were similar objects in the Department of Historical Studies at the nearby University of Malden. A little later it became clear that Adrian had seen these artefacts through the agency of his girlfriend who worked in a clerical position in that department. From there it was but a short step for the Examiners to be considering the possibility that Adrian had obtained his artefacts with connivance of his girlfriend. This had been strongly denied by Adrian.

Points for Consideration

- Should these connections have been detected earlier and the matter prevented from reaching the stage it has?
- To what extent should the supervisor be involved with the private life of the student?
- Should the supervisor have been aware of the possibility of relevant artefacts being present in a nearby institution?

After listening to this information, and with the agreement of both examiners, Dr Porteous made a call to the University of Malden and, after some initial difficulties, was able to ascertain from an older, retired member of the academic staff in the department of Historical Studies, that there was indeed a collection of artefacts there. According to his informant these had not been fully studied, largely because of concerns about their varied origin, queries with regard to both their initial discovery and their acquisition by the department many years ago. They had probably been untouched and unhandled for at least ten years.

Following receipt of this information, Dr Porteous and the examiners met together with Adrian, the Head of Department and the Graduate Tutor. Adrian continued to deny any suggestion of cheating, although the accusations from the examiners remained. Eventually it was agreed that all relevant individuals involved with the research project and the *viva* examination, along with representative(s) from the Department of Historical Studies at the University of Malden, should write reports on the matter, which would then be submitted to and dealt with by the university authorities, after which appropriate action would be taken. This would obviously be a prolonged and tortuous process, but was thought to be the correct way to proceed in this unhappy and salutary affair.

Points for Consideration

- What are the correct procedures to follow under these circumstances?
- What decision might be made about the outcome of the *viva* examination?
- Who should make this decision?
- Does this represent a case of 'poor' supervision?
- What steps should now be followed with regard to the student, and the supervisor?

Evolution of the problem

It is not usually possible, at the time of selection, to identify a student who is going to, or who might, should the opportunity and wherewithal arise, indulge in cheating in the research process.

The supervisor has possibly been too naïve in this situation. Through his contacts and knowledge of the field he should have been more scientifically critical and wary about the finds made by the student.

In the example described above, the student did appear to have problems progressing his research during the initial stages of his project, and closer contact between the student and his supervisor at the appropriate time might have averted the allegations of fraud.

Field notebooks at the archaeological site should have been meticulously kept, but there is no indication that they were carefully examined and signed off by the supervisor (or his deputy while he was on prolonged absence), together with the student, on a regular basis.

Out-of-hours-working should be carefully monitored, and a book for signing in and signing out by individuals, including students, should be readily and prominently available. It is bad practice, primarily for safety reasons, that a student (or staff member) be allowed to work alone out-of-hours.

Possible prevention and resolution of the problem

1. A full investigation of the matter along the lines indicated above undertaken by the university authorities with all concerned will be required. There are university regulations and guidelines governing the procedures to be followed.
2. Strict adherence to the procedures regarding out-of-hours working, and regular and closer monitoring by the supervisor of the student's notes could have reduced the opportunities for possible fraud to arise.
3. The supervisor could have been more closely attentive to the day-to-day

work of the student, and perhaps given greater scrutiny to the circumstances surrounding the disputed finds.

4. A supervisor with a research background more in tune with the research project would have a greater knowledge of any background associated with the work.

5. The problem has become a major one, but the gravity of the situation might have been avoided if the External Examiner had voiced his views and concerns to the supervisor prior to the *viva voce* examination.

6. Although this will be an uncommon situation, because of the prolonged problems in terms of reputations, careers affected, time involved, amount of administration it creates, litigation possibilities and departmental and institutional criticism that would be aroused, it is one that must remain at the back of a supervisor's mind.

29

An Issue of Collaboration

Scenario

Andrew Bright, a competent, confident, mature and responsible graduate student in the School of Management at the University of Redborough, was in the final year of his PhD programme and was preparing to undertake the write-up of his data. Andrew felt he had so far had a relatively smooth ride through his research studies, and, compared to some of his fellow students, considerable autonomy and freedom to pursue his work as seemed appropriate to him, with little imposed structure or close monitoring of his progress and pace. Although he had had meetings with all three members of his supervisory team, Dr Barnes, Professor Willis and Dr Gibson, these had been relatively infrequent, although it did not seem so, as he had three meetings to all other students one. On only two occasions, however, had Andrew met with all three of his supervisors together; once at the outset of his research studies, when his research question was defined and a possible research pathway outlined to him. During that meeting, there had been much animated discussion which Andrew had been unable to follow fully, but he had felt that, from what he could understand coupled with his own abilities, he would be able to cope with the work.

Points for Consideration

- Is it a good idea to have three, equally responsible, supervisors collaborating on a research programme for a single student?
- Could there be any logical reasons for the appointment of three supervisors?
- Would you consider the initial meeting between the student and all three supervisors to be a satisfactory one, and if not, why not?

His second meeting with all three supervisors together had taken place after his successful transfer almost a year later. The meeting had been quite short, but all three supervisors had expressed views that things were progressing well, that Andrew was clearly on track, and was a valuable student. Bringing the various and disparate threads of Andrew's research work together would, they all agreed, be a logical progression through his second year.

Andrew had seen each of his supervisors separately on a number of occasions through his second and third years, and these meetings had proved useful, but each supervisor had concentrated on their own particular area of expertise in relation to his research work. If Andrew had suggested that perhaps one supervisor might give an opinion or explain a point that appeared to be in the area of cognisance of another supervisor, or might perhaps support Andrew's contention that an important argument might be beneficial to his findings and provide a research direction that could overlap into the field of expertise of another supervisor, then the response he almost invariably received was that although it sounded very interesting, he should ask that question of the relevant supervisor.

Points for Consideration

- Is there sufficient, appropriate and useful collaboration between the three supervisors?
- Given that three supervisors are necessary for the research programme of this particular student, how might the supervisory arrangements have been improved?
- Would you expect an extremely competent student to be able to recognize and draw together the various aspects of his research without help?

As a consequence, Andrew had been left feeling somewhat exposed with regard to any clear, inter-reacting goals which his supervisors might be expecting him to aim for and achieve. He had to follow his own instincts and initiatives, and all through his second and final years these had seemed to be satisfactory as whenever he had presented his data and results to the appropriate supervisor, each had indicated to him that the outcome was satisfactory as far as they were concerned, although they often added that he should show his latest findings, and his interpretation of them, to both co-supervisors.

Point for Consideration

- Given that these rather over-complicated supervisory arrangements exist, who is responsible for organizing the required meetings between the supervisors and the student?

Because of the somewhat superficial and unfocused supervision he was receiving, Andrew's research had tended to follow different lines that intersected and impinged on one another to only a limited extent. Now, faced with putting his data together, he was finding it difficult to demonstrate, in his thesis write-up, the integration between the various aspects of his research. He had not been able to see any obvious, clear common theme to the work, as he was carrying out the research through the second and third years, and any common theme that had existed when he had started seemed to have disappeared. He'd been given somewhat diverse instructions from two of his co-supervisors about how to tackle the write-up (the third was away), but each had concentrated their advice on their own areas of expertise! Nevertheless, each had suggested he attempt to write the work in such a way as to provide some evidence of interdependence and cohesion between the various aspects of his research, but Andrew remained in great difficulties over this. Nevertheless, the date for his *viva voce* examination had been suggested for mid-December if he could submit his thesis on time, and it was clear to Andrew that he must push his write-up forward as rapidly as possible if he really wanted to take up a career opportunity early in the New Year. By early August, he had produced drafts of each of four data chapters (trying to link the work together where possible), and had also produced two differing drafts of an interpretative/discussion chapter, again attempting to integrate the information into some form of themed commonality.

Points for Consideration

- How might the student be best advised to undertake his write-up?
- Should all three supervisors be involved in advising and assisting with the write-up?
- What length of time should be allowed for the thesis write-up?
- Who has the primary responsibility for either initiating or progressing the write-up process?

Although he had worked hard at his write-up, Andrew had no way of knowing that what he had produced was what his supervisors wanted or was the best way of presenting his thesis information, and it was with some trepidation, therefore, that he handed his thesis chapter drafts to those two of his co-supervisors who were available in mid-August. His supervisor Professor Willis who had been away earlier had returned by now, but Dr Gibson was now away on holiday. It was about two weeks later that Andrew received separate e-mails almost simultaneously from both Dr Barnes and Professor Willis, demanding that he meet with each of them urgently. Andrew's response was to e-mail each of them suggesting a meeting between himself and both of them together. Not surprisingly such a meeting proved inordinately difficult to set up, and the only date they could come up with lay four weeks ahead, by which time Dr Gibson might also be available. Because of these time constraints, however, it was decided that Andrew would be advised to talk to each of the two available co-supervisors separately, so that he could progress with any modifications and alterations that his supervisors might propose for his thesis.

Point for Consideration

- How should the student respond to the supervisors' arrangements for the meetings at this late stage?

As it turned out, although Andrew was initially pleased to discover at the meetings with his supervisors that they had discussed his work with one another by telephone, and indicated to him how some interdependence and linking between the separate areas of his research could be interwoven into the presentation of his data, and also into his accompanying textual interpretation and discussion chapter, he was alarmed that both had proposed extensive changes to his draft chapters. In addition, neither supervisor felt competent to advise him on the absent supervisor's views of their joint write-up strategy, and indicated to Andrew that he would almost certainly need a third, modified version when it came to taking Dr Gibson's views into account.

Back at home, and sitting in front of his computer, Andrew was aghast as he contemplated the amount of work that would be involved in the alterations and reorganizations of his draft write-up that two of his supervisors had indicated should be carried out, not to mention the probability that his third supervisor would also require alterations to be made. Andrew wondered whether the changes Dr Gibson might request, which at best might necessitate some minor reorganizations, but at worst could take the form of an almost completely different accentuation being applied to the whole work and its interpretation, would trigger further demands for alteration from either Dr Barnes or Professor Willis, or from both of them. He decided his best option was to follow his own instinct, as he had done over the past two years, and which had served him in reasonably good stead.

Time was also pressing on, and he was due to submit his thesis in the next few weeks in order to meet his *viva voce* requirements. Accordingly he burnt the midnight oil over a three-week period and, with considerable difficulty, produced what he considered could be a compromise between his various research lines and their conclusions, and that also seemed to him to take account of the suggestions and advice he had already received from Dr Barnes and Professor Willis.

Points for Consideration

- Is the student wise to continue his write-up alone without seeking further help?
- Whom might he approach for assistance and what form might that assistance take?

> - Is it possible to postpone the date for a *viva* examination once it has been set?
> - If so, what repercussions might ensue and need to be considered?

By this time it was approaching mid-October, and all three of his supervisors were busy with their teaching duties, their new graduate students and the various administrative chores that the new Session brought. None of his supervisors approached Andrew, and it was left to him to contact each of them to inform them he had finished his write-up, and could they each have a look at it before he submitted it? His e-mails brought both predictable and unpredicted reactions; surprisingly Dr Gibson gave him the go-ahead to 'finish off the thesis with a careful proof-read', after which, as far as he was concerned, the thesis could be submitted. He added that he was really only a 'bit-player' in this work, and the main thrusts were coming from Barnes and Willis. Professor Willis, on the other hand, proved himself very concerned about the final version, which he termed a 'mish-mash of unsupported theorizing that failed to highlight and justify the most important and possibly fundamental points that the work had undoubtedly thrown up'. He also provided Andrew with a list of what he termed 'significant pointers' to help Andrew with his restructuring of the thesis.

Dr Barnes expressed himself satisfied in general terms with the presentation, but would have liked time to go through the work more thoroughly, and intimated that one or two of Andrew's interpretations looked a little precarious, but nevertheless, in his opinion, should be defensible.

After his corrected work had been returned, Andrew did not have a great deal of time to do anything more than give the thesis a final proof-read. To take Professor Willis's proposals into account would mean an almost complete rewrite and reorganization of at least three chapters, even if he, Andrew, had fully understood Professor Willis's wishes. Andrew therefore made what straightforward alterations he could, issued up a prayer, and took his thesis to the university's bindery.

Points for Consideration

- What more could the supervisors have done at this stage to help the student?
- What, if any, alternative options are open to the student?
- Who should take overall responsibility for the submission of the thesis at this stage?

On a cold, misty and overcast afternoon in December, Andrew underwent his *viva voce* ordeal. None of his supervisors were anywhere to be seen. The examination was not a success. Both his examiners felt the thesis was difficult to come to grips with; much of the interpretation was muddled; some of the information provided had not been properly evaluated, or worse, totally overlooked; the overall research strategy that had been stated in the Aims and Objectives was mired, and almost unrecognizable through the main body of the thesis; the thesis did not represent a cohesive body of the work and there was no all-embracing pattern to the presentation. In spite of this, the examiners felt the actual research had been adequately performed and had given rise to some intriguing findings that had, nevertheless, not as yet been fully substantiated. The problems of the submission lay almost entirely in the presentation of the thesis. They recommended the thesis be re-written and re-submitted within one year. Andrew was devastated and went straight out to drown his sorrows.

Points for Consideration

- How much contact should take place between the supervisor and the Internal Examiner in arranging the *viva* examination, and in considering the student's thesis submission and his position *vis-à-vis* the supervisor(s)?

- Should any, or all three, of the supervisors have been available to support the student on the day of the *viva* examination?

- At this point in the process, and following the decision of the examiners, has the student any redress?

Evolution of the problem

Although the use of three supervisors collaborating on the research programme of a single student represents a slightly more unusual scenario, the use of more than one supervisor to supervise a single student, without any indication who is the lead supervisor can create problems for the student both during the progress of the PhD, and at the stage of thesis write-up.

Although all collaborating supervisors met with the student on two occasions during his PhD programme, on neither occasion did they ensure that the student fully understood the details of the strategies, themes and lines of research he was being asked to pursue.

No individual supervisor showed any wish to take responsibility for the student's overall progress, and to co-ordinate the student's research findings. There was a lack of clear research direction provided by the supervisors. These matters were accentuated by the failure on the part of the supervisors to become properly involved to take responsibility or to identify one of them to take overall responsibility for the student's thesis write-up.

The supervisors properly appreciated the competence of the student, but, perhaps because of their own individual agendas in respect of his research programme, did not fully consider the difficulties that would need to be overcome in integrating the varying lines of research, particularly at the time of the thesis write-up. The supervisors overestimated the capabilities of the student.

There was a lack of close, careful supervision throughout the PhD in terms of a lack of meetings between all protagonists, ensuring the student was fully cognizant of intricacies and the integrative nature of his work, and in general supervisor support and guidance.

No information or guidance for the student to assist with the thesis write-up was provided throughout the three-year research programme.

The student failed to bring his situation to the attention of the Graduate Tutor as soon as he realized that problems were arising for him.

Prevention and possible resolution of the problem

1. For any PhD research programme involving supervisor collaboration it is important to identify a lead supervisor who has overall responsibility for the progress of the work and who sets up a working relationship with the student.
2. Even when a joint collaboration between two supervisors, both of whom will be making equal contributions to the research strategy and its progress over the duration of a PhD programme, is undertaken, then one of them must be identified as the lead supervisor who has clear responsibility for working with the student and also liaising closely with the co-supervisor.
3. Meetings between all supervisors involved and the student should take place regularly, and at a frequency that ensures all individuals involved are aware of and fully understand what the research programme involves, how it is progressing, and what problems are emerging.
4. Even an extremely competent or mature research student would be hard-pressed to write up a PhD thesis without considerable advice and input from a supervisor. With two supervisors, meetings between both of them without the student may be useful to clarify research themes and strategies, identify and solve problems arising in the research, and to determine approaches and strategies for the thesis write-up. With three supervisors, such meetings must take place. In both cases the information and outcomes from such meetings are transmitted to and discussed with the student by the lead supervisor.
5. Before the time for the thesis write-up, the student should be asked to submit some form of written thesis material to the lead supervisor, who may then be able to gauge the writing abilities of the student and gain some estimate of the writing (and correcting) time that will be required.
6. The student could have aired his concerns and worries about supervisory difficulties with the Graduate Tutor on at least two occasions; as he realized in his second year that the collaborative supervision was not working satisfactorily, and prior to the commencement of his thesis write-up in his final year. In both instances the Graduate Tutor would be expected to

speak to the supervisors and resolve the problem by identifying a lead supervisor.

7. When the difficulties with the write-up remain unrecognized until a late stage, it is wise to postpone the *viva* examination. This is possible and can be organized by the supervisor through the Internal Examiner. However, in most circumstances it is realized that a *viva* date will not be set until after thesis submission, for precisely the reason that it is difficult to accurately predict the submission date.

8. One of the supervisors in the Issue described here must have taken responsibility for selection of the examiners and liaising with the student and the Internal Examiner on the *viva* date. More enlightened discussion between the individuals involved at this stage would have highlighted the problems and resulted in solutions put in place at the time, thereby avoiding the final disastrous outcome.

9. The problems that may arise through postponing the *viva* examination may be the availability of the examiners; student career prospects; student commitments and travelling arrangements; university PhD submission and completion rates.

10. The final submission of the thesis is the responsibility of the student. Once the student has completed the write-up to the satisfaction of the supervisor, and has been made aware of the date of the *viva* examination and the names of the examiners, the responsibilities of the supervisor towards the student are over. However, in normal circumstances, the student's supervisor or lead supervisor in a collaborative venture would both wish and expect to be present to provide whatever support might be required on the day of the *viva* examination.

11. The lack of identified responsibility was in all probability the reason for failure of the supervisors to support the student on the day of the *viva*. This would have been resolved through the intervention of the Graduate Tutor, provided the supervisory problem had been brought to their attention.

12. The student has no redress regarding the lack of supervisor presence and support on the day of his *viva* examination. However, if a complaint regarding the quality of the supervision is deemed necessary by the student, then this could be lodged, if only to raise awareness of the particular problems experienced in this scenario, at this point in time.

30

An Issue of Procedure

Scenario

Adrienne felt intellectually battered and completely drained physically after her *viva* examination. She had never expected it to last as long as it had, almost four-and-a-half hours, and could not understand why it should have been so protracted.

Points for Consideration

- Should there be limitations on the length of the *viva* examination?
- Should there be guidance on the conduct of the *viva* examination in general?
- Might the student have been more prepared for the *viva* experience?

At the same time she was incredibly relieved that at last it was all over and that the outcome seemed to her to have been a reasonably positive one. With a complete chapter to restructure, some references to insert and a manageable number of suggested minor alterations, together with correction of typographical errors that the examiners had apparently agreed following the prolonged discussion they had after Adrienne had been asked to leave at the end of the *viva*, it seemed that they would, after all, recommend the award of her doctorate. When she emerged mentally battered and bruised after her *viva*, her supervisor had suggested they meet the day after next to discuss the date she would be required to complete the alterations, and the best way to proceed with these requirements. Although elated, Adrienne also felt somewhat dissatisfied with the conduct and her whole experience of the *viva* examination she had gone through. However, she resolved to forget that for the moment, and to look forward to enjoying a celebratory meal with her partner that evening.

The following day, reflecting on her experiences, Adrienne felt amazed at the final outcome of the *viva*, which seemed at variance, and somewhat inconsistent with the very negative and intimidating reception her research work had received from Professor Perry, her External Examiner. Things had not gone well from the outset, and at the commencement of the *viva*, Professor Perry had undertaken his examiner role with considerable gusto, and with what seemed to Adrienne, unnecessary aggression and forcefulness, and the challenges to, and rapid-fire questioning about her research data and manner of presentation had come thick and fast. Adrienne had responded by both explaining and providing, as she saw it, justification for her research methodology and for the interpretation of her results, but Professor Perry had brushed aside, trivialized, and had certainly not accepted her responses. Using a hostile and sniping approach, or so it seemed to Adrienne, he had repeatedly questioned the validity of some of the qualitative data in her research and seemed to imply that Adrienne's conclusions were not at all justified by her data, at least with respect to one section of her work in particular. He continually reverted to questioning this part of her research, drawing attention to what he seemed to feel was, in one or two instances at least, its very subjective nature.

Points for Consideration

- How is the selection of examiners for a PhD carried out?
- Is the approach of the External Examiner to this *viva* an acceptable one?
- What is an External Examiner assessing in the *viva voce* examination?

As the *viva* progressed, it had seemed to Adrienne that most of the responses she had made were met with yet further questions on exactly the same issues. Admittedly, Dr Porter, the Internal Examiner, while rigorous in her examination of the research, had shown a much more conciliatory and fair approach and had appeared to find Adrienne's explanations and justifications of her strategic approach, interpretations of, and conclusions to her work very acceptable. However, this had had no impact on either Professor Perry's lines of questioning, or on his forceful, cynical and sarcastic manner.

Points for Consideration

- What should be the role of the Internal Examiner in the PhD examination?
- Is it possible, or indeed advisable, to involve the supervisor at any stage of the *viva voce* examination?

As the *viva* examination progressed, Adrienne had felt increasingly intimidated and bullied by Professor Perry's approach as well as what seemed to be insinuations that the perspectives which informed the research were less than adequate.

Points for Consideration

- In this situation is the Internal Examiner entitled to call for some sort of control in the *viva voce* examination process?
- Has the student any rights at this stage?
- If so, how should the student proceed?

Adrienne had also, at times, thought that they were going round in circles with questions repeatedly covering the same issues. Occasional glances at, and eye contact with, the Internal Examiner had seemed to suggest that she was also finding the situation rather uncomfortable. Adrienne reflected on how stressed she had been during the entire examination, but that neither she, nor the Internal Examiner had seemed able to do anything about it; even a visit to the toilet had not appeared to be an option!

Points for Consideration

- Is it the duty of the examiner to ensure that a student whose career will be in research should be shown the high and rigorous standards required in this type of work?
- Is this approach an important part of the *viva* and the PhD experience?
- Can the student make a formal complaint about the conduct of the *viva voce* examination?

At the meeting with her supervisor the following day, Adrienne voiced her views about the length and tone of her *viva* ordeal and enquired whether this kind of experience was normal in a *viva voce* examination. She explained her concerns over the robust, almost scornful and intimidating questioning she had received, and the impression she had also had, that her work was being disparaged and derided. Was her research or its presentation really as poor as the External Examiner had seemed to imply, and, if so, why had her supervisor encouraged her to present her results in the first place, and how had she managed to be awarded the PhD? She even went so far as to indicate to her supervisor that she felt so numbed and upset by the whole experience, which she perceived to have been traumatic and degrading, that she was considering lodging a complaint about the conduct of the examination and, indeed, about the behaviour and arrogance of her External Examiner. Adrienne's supervisor said he thought that would be unwise; the *viva* examination system in the United Kingdom had taken this form for many years, and although nowadays there was usually a more easy-going and 'user-friendly' attitude towards PhD *vivas* by examiners, there was still the odd, traditional or inexperienced examiner around who believed it was necessary to conduct a confrontational and attacking approach in the examination to establish the student's mental activity, and ability to defend a stated viewpoint. In any case, Adrienne was going to get her PhD with just a little more work on the thesis, and it was perhaps inadvisable to create issues following her experience, when in all probability nothing would be achieved. Privately, he thought he would not ask Professor Perry to act as an External Examiner again. His brief discussion on the previous day with the Internal Examiner had not allayed his concerns. Dr Porter had indicated to him that Professor Perry had indeed been a hard examiner, but had identified certain flaws in Adrienne's work which he was at pains to focus Adrienne's attention to in the *viva*. According to Dr Porter, however, Adrienne had failed to see and understand the points and interpretations that Professor Perry was getting at, and it was this that had irritated the External Examiner. In Dr Porter's opinion, Adrienne was lucky to get away without having to undergo resubmission.

Points for Consideration

- Do you think a correct decision has been reached for the outcome of this *viva* examination?
- What remarks might the supervisor address to the student with respect to the outcome of the examination?

Evolution of the problem

The student was probably not consulted on the choice of examiners, and although the supervisor is in the best position to make the selection, there may be circumstances where the student has some views on the matter.

There was a lack of preparation on the part of the student for the experience of the *viva voce* examination. No information and advice had been given to the student on how the *viva voce* examination was likely to be conducted. The extreme length of the *viva* contributed to the student's concerns with the *viva* procedures.

There was no effective intervention by the Internal Examiner to control the *viva* examination, and prevent the procedures getting out of hand. The role of the Internal Examiner is to ensure that the External Examiner's analysis, understanding and appraisal of the student's work are rigorous and fair. The External Examiner, while undoubtedly doing his job, showed an unwarranted lack of courtesy and unsympathetic appreciation of the student's position.

Procedures differ between institutions, but in most, the supervisor plays no role in the examination procedure. The student's rights during the actual examination are unclear, but most examiners would permit a student to visit the washroom if the *viva* is becoming a protracted one.

It is unfortunate when, for the student, what should be an enjoyable *viva* experience, expounding on the details of, and the views generated from, their research work, and demonstrating to a 'captive audience' the fruits of a successful training in research, turns out to be an extremely unpleasant one.

The student should not lodge a formal complaint. The grounds for her doing so are somewhat tenuous if the Internal Examiner's views are correct, and although there was undoubtedly evidence for an overbearing, discourteous and inconsiderate manner on the part of the External Examiner, it appears as though he was doing his job, and may in fact have given the student the benefit of the doubt and shown leniency in making the decision to recommend award of the PhD.

Possible prevention and resolution of the problem

1. The selection of the examiners should involve both the student and the supervisor, and the supervisor should explain the rationale behind the selection of the examiners (usually complementing one another in their approach to the student's work) to the student. The supervisor, in making the selection of examiners, should take into account any strong views of the student on the proposed choice.
2. The student should be provided with information about the possible approaches that may be used by the examiners to probe and assess the student's research strategy, approach, understanding, interpretation and presentation of the work, and to ensure the student is fully versed in research methodology.
3. The make-up of the examining panel (External and Internal Examiner) should also be considered by the supervisor in making the selection. An experienced Internal Examiner may counterbalance a difficult, aggressive, prejudiced or egotistical External Examiner, and be in a position to minimize the potentially uncomfortable situation for a student who is enduring a confrontational, discourteous or unfair examination procedure.
4. The student must be made aware that a rigorous approach is required in undertaking research and examiners may themselves adopt a strong and aggressive approach to explore and assess the student's research abilities and their understanding of the rigorous nature of research, in the *viva* examination.
5. Although the supervisor should not support the student in lodging a formal complaint, the manner in which the *viva* examination was conducted, and the student's views could be brought to the attention of the university authorities by a letter from the supervisor. The supervisor should inform the student of the line of action which will be taken and the student must be informed as to any outcome of this action.
6. The student should be brought to realize that there were flaws in their PhD work or its presentation, and that the student's failure to recognize

these may have been the reason for the irascibility of the External Examiner. The Examiners may have been concerned that when the student failed to pick up on these problems with the work, it made it more difficult for them to realize a successful outcome for the PhD. The inability of the student to recognize the possible validity of an alternative viewpoint, and to discuss this viewpoint rationally, logically and in depth, could be taken to represent a failure in the research training that should be provided by the PhD through the supervisor.

31

Conclusions

In the preceding Issues, several key themes have emerged and these will be discussed here. As an interactive exercise, a Key Question has been extracted from every Issue and these are listed at the end of this section. Considered responses to these Key Questions can be found in Appendix 1.

Not surprisingly, there is a certain amount of overlap between the key themes and the Key Questions. Where this occurs, these particular themes will not be discussed in detail.

English language competency

For overseas students in particular, two important considerations at the stage of application for entry to a higher degree research programme, are whether non-UK qualifications meet UK standards and how a student is best judged to be suitably competent with the English language. For the former, there will be varying processes of comparative assessment at different institutions, while for the latter, institutional bodies such as the International Office and English Language Teaching Centre can provide extra help and advice.

Student–supervisor expectations

In the Introduction a number of expectations which the student and supervisor might reasonably seek from one another were listed. These lists are not intended to be comprehensive, but do provide some indication of the variety of expectations that different students may have of their supervisor and of the supervisory process.

Perhaps the most important fact to remember when a new research student commences a programme of work, is for the supervisor to have an introductory meeting with the student, to indicate exactly what expectations the supervisor has of them. At such an early stage of the research programme however, it is probably too soon in most instances for the student to do likewise. However, the student–supervisor relationship should develop so that later in the programme, and ideally at some point in the first six months, the student can be encouraged to discuss what expectations they have of the supervisor.

Because each student will probably have different expectations, it is vital that appropriate dialogue takes place between student and supervisor at an early stage.

MPhil/PhD transfer

As indicated in a number of the Issues, the transfer from an MPhil to PhD, or from an MPhil to MD, is an important early milestone of progress in a research programme. Its usefulness now lies in the more formal and rigorous procedures used for assessment in most institutions, such as a transfer report and mini-*viva*, both examined by a panel of academics which may or may not include the supervisor. As well as ensuring that appropriate standards in research are being achieved, the MPhil/PhD transfer also places emphasis on management of research time. In the past, at the beginning of any research programme the impression often given was that thesis submission was many years away, and because of this, progress could be slow in the first year. New procedures introduced for the MPhil transfer now place greater emphasis on short-term goals which should improve the overall efficiency and focus of the research.

Communication between student and supervisor

In an ideal situation, considerations as to how and when communication should take place between student and supervisor could be addressed when respective expectations are being discussed. This may not be an issue in situations where students see their supervisors on a regular basis. However, it can be more problematic with part-time students, students working away from the university and in disciplines where students see their supervisors only rarely. In these situations, a busy supervisor can easily forget a student's timescale of events.

Some type of system and frequency of regular communication should therefore be maintained if at all possible and this will be facilitated if the supervisor and student have established and can adhere to a regular meetings timetable.

Supervisory meetings and record keeping

This is an area where significant developments have taken place in the past few years. Recording of formal meetings, which should take place every four to eight weeks depending on circumstances, is a useful way of monitoring student progress. Nowadays, with increasing numbers of student appeals being brought against supervisors, a record of meetings when signed by both parties, not only indicates that they have taken place, but also provides detailed documentation of the progress of the student in question. It is particularly useful if the frequency of meetings can be agreed early in the programme but with sufficient flexibility built in to allow, for example, for an increased frequency of meetings should this be considered necessary.

Student independence

One of the main goals for a student undertaking a research degree is that they themselves develop into independent researchers. Part of the supervisor's responsibility is to help them achieve this aim as they see fit. This is just one reason why it should be an advantage for a student to have an experienced supervisor. Again there will be extremes between students with respect to their approach to research, such as those who want to do their own research in year one, to those who have not achieved research independence by year three. Although there are various ways for supervisors to engender independence in students during the research degree process, it is highly desirable that the supervisor gets to know the student well enough, to allow for different strategies and timescales to be used in aiming for this goal for each individual student.

Student motivation

Perhaps one of the biggest causes of frustration and disappointment for a student in the research process is when nothing seems to be going right with their research programme and they feel they are making no headway. At times like these, the student needs support and guidance in attempting to progress the work, and under these circumstances the experience of the supervisor in setting the research programme back on track is often invaluable, and occasionally vital. A supervisor's ability to achieve this as tactfully as possible is particularly desirable.

At other times, however, it has to be remembered that it may not be the research programme that is the problem, but that other factors such as personal problems of the student may be affecting the work, and must also be considered.

Finally, albeit only rarely, the research undertaking itself might be responsible for the lack of motivation. In some cases it is not until the student begins a research programme that they realize the research process is not for them. It is clearly advantageous for both parties if such students can be identified at an early stage and encouraged to leave.

Second supervisors

Even though the new Code of Practice on Postgraduate Research Programmes (QAA 2004) recommends that each student has a minimum of one main supervisor, it acknowledges that normally this supervisor will be part of a supervisory team. It is of course essential for a replacement supervisor to be found, especially should the principal supervisor be absent for a significant period of time. Moreover, a student may be experiencing problems with their main supervisor and in that situation an additional supervisor who takes on a more pastoral role might be able to help out, possibly in liaison with the departmental Graduate Tutor and/or Head of Department. With this in mind, it becomes highly unlikely that a student will have only a single supervisor. A more recent development has been a general recommendation that inexperienced supervisors have an experienced supervisor or mentor to co-supervise at least their first research student. This allows the inexperienced supervisor the opportunity to gain supervisory skills and experience, without disadvantaging the student.

Graduate Tutor

A Graduate Tutor is usually the person in a department who oversees, and sometimes manages the procedures put into place for monitoring research student progress. This often includes an involvement with transfer procedures. Normally, the Graduate Tutor is also a source of information on guidelines with respect to all aspects of the research supervisory process, as they often chair departmental Graduate Research Committees and serve on Faculty and/or University Graduate Research Committees.

In addition, Graduate Tutors, because of their knowledge and experience, may often be consulted by students and/or supervisors in the event of a breakdown, or impending breakdown, in the student–supervisor relationship. It is of course desirable for a Graduate Tutor to be consulted at an early stage in such cases to prevent irrecoverable damage to the relationship.

Head of Department

Like the Graduate Tutor, the Head of Department also has a responsibility towards both students and staff. A notable difference, however, is that while a Graduate Tutor acts in an advisory capacity, the Head of Department often has ultimate responsibility in decision-making that may directly affect both student and supervisor. The Head of Department may also be influential in helping less experienced supervisors and may be instrumental in developing departmental policy towards research student recruitment, numbers of students taken on for research programmes within the department, and enlightened allocation of students to supervisors.

Ideally, a good Head of Department will have both an interest in, and a general awareness of, developments in graduate education with the aim of improving the quality of research student supervision and research student completion times.

Thesis writing

When taking into account different practices of thesis preparation among various disciplines within the university, it is probably true to say that, in general, students now are better prepared for writing their theses. This is because of extra demands on the transfer procedure and increased pressure on students to publish at least some of their research before the thesis is submitted. Additional help is on hand today in most universities from Research Training Programme (RTP) modules and additional skills training in this area.

Viva voce

Not so long ago, the *viva voce* examination was shrouded in mystery and any actual preparation for the event itself was limited or even non-existent. At present, the *viva*, although still daunting for the student, has become somewhat more open and 'user-friendly', with the student being consulted, in many institutions, in the selection of the examiners, provided with some information about what to expect during the examination process, and even given a 'mock' *viva*, although this is still the exception rather than the rule. Furthermore, there are now comprehensive texts in the areas of thesis writing and *viva voce* preparation which can be consulted. In spite of this, the *viva* remains an unregulated and uncontrolled form of examination, but is generally accepted by all concerned as being an important platform for the student to defend their thesis research work as set out in their thesis, thereby demonstrating a variety of skills needed in the research arena.

Complaints and appeals

Students now, quite rightly, expect good supervision, and should this not be forthcoming, they are more likely to lodge complaints with the appropriate body. If, after considerable investment in time and money by all concerned, a student fails a research degree and considers that the quality of their supervision, for example, has played some role in this, then nowadays, they are much more likely to formulate complaints and appeal against the decision.

The message here is while the overall quality of supervision has probably increased over the last few years, the consequences of poor or inadequate supervision have become more serious. Therefore, with support for improving the quality of supervision increasing both locally and nationally, it is important that we take advantage of these opportunities to raise still further our standards of research student supervision. A three- or four-year research programme is an expensive and lengthy process, and this investment of time and money by all participants, to say nothing of the career prospects of the individual student, the value to the country as a whole of the expertise gained, and the marketable assets of a successfully trained research worker, are incalculable. It behoves all involved as supervisors of research students to ensure that the outcomes are successful.

Key Questions

1. *An Issue of Isolation* – How can a new research student be prepared for the difference in lifestyle as a postgraduate?
2. *An Issue of Conflict* – Following a major dispute between supervisor and student, how can a reasonable working relationship be re-established?
3. *An Issue of Non-Compliance* – Who decides what the research project will be about?
4. *An Issue of Plagiarism* – How best can a supervisor recognize signs of plagiarism?
5. *An Issue of Time* – Can a part-time student ever be other than an isolated and independent researcher?
6. *An Issue of Language* – Can an overseas student's competence in English be assessed adequately at the application stage?
7. *An Issue of Writing* – How many times can a research student reasonably be expected to attempt the transfer procedure?
8. *An Issue of Scrutiny* – Should there be any mechanisms in place to assess the feasibility of a research programme?
9. *An Issue of Transfer* – What are the advantages of a supervisory meeting log?
10. *An Issue of Progress* – How does a supervisor maintain student motivation and ensure continuity in the progress of the work?
11. *An Issue of Judgement* – What are the boundaries of responsibility towards an overseas research student?
12. *An Issue of Distance* – If good supervision arises out of a close working relationship with the student, does supervision of a remote location student always have to be compromised?
13. *An Issue of Teaching* – Is it a good idea for a student to get involved in departmental teaching?
14. *An Issue of Management* – Must a student have confidence in their supervisor's abilities to complete a research programme?
15. *An Issue of Culture* – Is it generally true that overseas students are less likely to demonstrate independence in their research?

16. *An Issue of Funding* – If a student experiences financial difficulties, what should a supervisor advise?
17. *An Issue of Appeal* – How involved should a supervisor become with a student when the latter experiences personal problems?
18. *An Issue of Stability* – If a supervisor obtains a position elsewhere, what is their responsibility towards their research student?
19. *An Issue of Ownership* – Who owns the work performed by a research student?
20. *An Issue of Availability* – What should be the extent of supervisor involvement and support at different stages of a doctoral research programme?
21. *An Issue of Health* – How long can a student be registered for a research degree?
22. *An Issue of Direction* – At what point might a student be considered capable of working independently?
23. *An Issue of Contract* – Who bears the ultimate responsibility associated with the PhD write-up and submission?
24. *An Issue of Priority* – After a research student has completed their research, taken up employment but still has not written the thesis, whose responsibility is it to get it finished?
25. *An Issue of Write-Up* – At what point does a supervisor decide that there is sufficient research content for thesis completion?
26. *An Issue of* Viva *Preparation* – Should all research students be offered a mock *viva*?
27. *An Issue of Identity* – How much involvement should a student have in the choice of External Examiner?
28. *An Issue of Alleged Fraud* – What are the disadvantages of a student having only one supervisor?
29. *An Issue of Collaboration* – Increasingly, students are being allocated more than one supervisor. How can a student be managed optimally by a supervisory team?
30. *An Issue of Procedure* – What is the role of the Internal Examiner in the *viva* and its aftermath?

Appendix 1: Answers to the Key Questions

In the discussion chapter a key question was identified for each of the case studies. The aim of this appendix is to present our considered opinions to each question, with reference wherever possible to the new Code of Practice (QAA 2004) as described in the Introduction.

1. *An Issue of Isolation – How can a new research student be prepared for the difference in lifestyle as a postgraduate?*
   It can certainly be useful if the new student is in a situation where advice can be sought from more experienced students, ideally in the same department. In some institutions the idea of a student mentor is a good one where a more senior student gives time to help a new student settle in over a period of several months. From a more academic standpoint, wide-ranging support provided by several departmental (for example, seminars) and possibly faculty activities (for example, workshops) in addition to that provided by the supervisor could be useful. A particularly good way of helping a student is to ask them to find out as much as they can about what research students do before taking up a position. Hopefully, good preparation will reduce the incidence and intensity of bad experiences.

2. *An Issue of Conflict – Following a major dispute between supervisor and student, how can a reasonable working relationship be re-established?*
   To some extent, this partly depends on the nature of the dispute. If, however, the basis of the dispute was conflict, it would seem reasonable to involve a third party such as the Graduate Tutor to bring the two parties together for discussions. Through these discussions it would then become clear whether a working relationship could be re-established or not. If not, then alternative supervisory arrangements would have to be made. If both parties agreed to continue, ideally a second supervisor might be appointed and it would probably be a good idea for the Graduate Tutor to be updated at regular intervals. Completion of a supervisory meeting log would be essential.

3. *An Issue of Non-Compliance – Who decides what the research project will be about?*
This depends somewhat on the discipline. For example, in the Arts a student may have funding to work in a general topic area and the supervisor has to be matched to the appropriate field. It is likely that a certain amount of flexibility might be allowed to develop the research area as long as the supervisor was comfortable with the way the project was going. In the Sciences, supervisors usually offer projects in very specific subjects and there would be little flexibility to move around the specific topic. In this particular Issue, funding was provided to the supervisor to work on a very specific topic and by agreeing to work on this project, the student has to understand that there can be little or no deviation from this.

4. *An Issue of Plagiarism – How best can a supervisor recognize signs of plagiarism?*
There are several potential indicators of plagiarism. First, if a supervisor knows the literature well enough, it is easy to identify copying from specific sources. Second, when a student describes their work, in the context of the known literature, different styles of writing are often apparent, sometimes with different spellings. Finally, in a student oral presentation sometimes their work may be poorly described and this can contrast quite markedly with their possibly plagiarized, lucid written work.

5. *An Issue of Time – Can a part-time student ever be other than an isolated and independent researcher?*
This depends very much on the discipline and how a research student's programme of study is managed. In some subject areas such as the Arts, full-time students may often feel isolated and the ability to work independently is essential. What is of importance in these situations is that the supervisor keeps in close contact with the student, normally on a regular basis, if this is what the student desires. For disciplines in which a supervisor may not meet with students that often, it probably doesn't make any difference whether a student is part-time or full-time. However, in the Sciences, for example, where students often work in research groups, and usually see their supervisor on a daily basis, a part-time student because of their employment commitments works more independently on their research project, and under normal circumstances would see their supervisor only occasionally. If it can be achieved, an ideal solution would be to try and get the part-time student working together with the supervisor's research group whenever possible.

6. *An Issue of Language – Can an overseas student's competence in English be assessed adequately at the application stage?*
Ideally, all prospective postgraduate research students should be interviewed. However, if this is not possible (which may often be the case with overseas applicants), one has to rely on approved assessments such as the Test of English as a Foreign Language (TOEFL) or International English Language Testing System (IELTS) scores. With increasing pressures on the quality of research degrees and thesis submission rates, it is important that a research student has few weaknesses in English. Therefore, the

trend is for greater expectations of English competency as reflected in higher TOEFL or IELTS scores. Any compromise in this area could result in a student making poor progress.

7. *An Issue of Writing – How many times can a research student reasonably be expected to attempt the transfer procedure?*
This should, of course, be determined by institutional regulations and/or departmental guidelines. However, from time to time these may need changing and it would be a good idea if one could justify current procedures. From our experience, we believe that unless there are extenuating circumstances, such as illness and/or resource implications, it is in the student's best interests if a failed transfer attempt is given only one more chance, typically after a period of six months for a full-time student. Pressures on submission rates, realistically, do not normally allow for students to be considering transfer towards the end of their second academic year.

8. *An Issue of Scrutiny – Should there be any mechanisms in place to assess the feasibility of a research programme?*
There should not be any problems for projects that are peer-reviewed externally, for example by granting bodies. However, although some supervisors might feel undermined if their academic judgement is questioned, internal peer-review of proposed research projects should improve quality overall. Therefore, peer-review of all research proposals should be strongly recommended.

9. *An Issue of Transfer – What are the advantages of a supervisory meeting log?*
Completion of a supervisory meeting log on a regular basis allows both student and supervisor to be aware of a student's progress and for targets to be set. It also provides a record of meetings which could be of use if a student complained of a lack of supervision. It is perhaps of little consequence whether the student or supervisor completes the log, as long as it is signed by both parties and a correct record is kept.

10. *An Issue of Progress – How does a supervisor maintain student motivation and ensure continuity in the progress of the work?*
It is expected that the supervisor will maintain frequent and regular contact with the student, providing encouragement and constructive criticism. Whatever happens during the research programme, the student should not lose sight of both the short-term and long-term goals of the research project. Similarly, realistic timescales set at the commencement of the research programme should be known and understood by the student.

11. *An Issue of Judgement – What are the boundaries of responsibility towards an overseas research student?*
In some situations when overseas students have government scholarships, these scholarships are awarded to students to follow a defined path of study. In everybody's interests it would not be advisable to accept such students unless their specific project requirements could be met. In all cases, clarification of the research project is essential at an early stage.

However, it should be recognized by all parties that, by their very nature, research projects often develop in ways that are not anticipated at the outset. If the intended project is not performed, not only is this bad news for the student, but it is also likely that such government scholarship students would be advised in future not to apply to such institutions that fail to fulfil the wishes of the scholarship.

12. *An Issue of Distance – If good supervision arises out of a close working relationship with the student, does supervision of a remote location student always have to be compromised?*

    Certainly, opportunities for a supervisor to develop a close working relationship with a remote location student are reduced when compared to a full-time student. However, depending on the efforts and the personality of both supervisor and student, and quality of communication between the two, there should be ample opportunity for a good working relationship to develop. This could be enhanced further if the student and/or supervisor have the opportunity to meet face-to-face during the research programme. It is, of course, always possible that the institution and its staff are already known to the supervisor, which could also be advantageous.

13. *An Issue of Teaching – Is it a good idea for a student to get involved in departmental teaching?*

    This depends on the student and how the teaching is managed. Many students like to engage in some form of teaching as it often broadens their experience as well as providing a minor financial incentive. If a relatively small amount of teaching is performed by the student who has received appropriate training, then the experience should be entirely beneficial. However, what is not wanted is a significant demand on research time caused by excessive teaching in a non-supportive environment without a mentor. Such a situation could easily get out of hand and become problematic.

14. *An Issue of Management – Must a student have confidence in their supervisor's abilities to complete a research programme?*

    One of a research student's expectations of a supervisor is that they should demonstrate knowledge and expertise in the chosen research field. Without this, not surprisingly, many students would be concerned at the quality of supervision. However, this situation can be helped by a knowledgeable co-supervisor. Also, an experienced and successful supervisor can often make up for certain deficiencies in subject knowledge. Nevertheless, the importance of a student's lack of confidence in their supervisor should not be underestimated.

    Moreover, expressing this opinion to a personal tutor or Graduate Tutor would be quite difficult for a student and therefore should be taken very seriously.

15. *An Issue of Culture – Is it generally true that overseas students are less likely to demonstrate independence in their research?*

    Any student who is new to a university, and perhaps more so to a new country, will for a while show greater dependency on the supervisor. However, as time progresses this dependency should lessen. One needs to realize that the term overseas student applies to people from all over the world, and regarding culture, it is impossible to make generalizations. It is true some overseas students, because of their cultural background, will show less independence in their research, while others from a different cultural background, may show greater independence in their research compared to the average UK student.

For a supervisor, cultural awareness and getting to know the student are vital for better student management.

16. *An Issue of Funding – If a student experiences financial difficulties, what should a supervisor advise?*
If the student experiences minor short-term financial difficulties, universities are usually quite sympathetic and arrangements can be made so as to lessen the problem. Often Student Services or a similar body should be informed and advice given is usually sufficient to address the problem successfully. If, however, the student experiences a major longer-term financial difficulty, it may well be in everyone's interest to allow the student a Leave of Absence so that sufficient time is given to try and solve this problem. If this problem cannot be addressed then, unless a student is coming to the end of the research programme, it is more likely that the student's registration will be terminated. Although this decision seems harsh, in the past too many supervisors have tried to keep the student working, often in very difficult circumstances, where considerable pressure has been put on the student, which often leads to further academic and personal problems.

17. *An Issue of Appeal – How involved should a supervisor become with a student when the latter experiences personal problems?*
A supervisor can be sympathetic and understanding when a student experiences personal problems. However, on the whole it is probably safer to recommend that the student seeks institutional help. This means that other people are involved apart from the supervisor and could provide guidance to the latter as how best to proceed in the interests of the student. As in other relationships, not getting too close to a student allows the supervisor to be more objective should difficult decisions need to be made. Moreover, from a simple time management point of view, many supervisors would not have the time (or the expertise) to give to a student who may be experiencing major difficulties.

18. *An Issue of Stability – If a supervisor obtains a position elsewhere, what is their responsibility towards their research student?*
Once a supervisor leaves their place of employment, they have no official responsibility towards a student as a student's registration and supervision should relate to the same university. If, however, a supervisor moved to another university, then a student might in some circumstances be given the opportunity to complete their research at the new institution, as long as funding was not an issue. If the student had almost completed

the research, then the original supervisor, if they so wished, could continue as unofficial supervisor in addition to a new lead supervisor being appointed. The latter situation would be easier and continuity maintained if students always had more than one supervisor.

19. *An Issue of Ownership – Who owns the work performed by a research student?*
   In some areas such as the sciences and engineering, ownership of the work produced by a student has taken on greater importance in recent years. Certainly in some institutions, students are required to write up all experiments in a laboratory book which is signed off by the supervisor. At the completion of the project, the laboratory books remain the property of the university and although students are able to consult them, they cannot usually be taken away. Where research is being sponsored by a commercial organization, ownership is usually governed by contractual agreement.

   Apart from thesis submission, responsibility for publication of any research carried out under their supervision is that of the supervisor, although appropriate credit should be given to the student if they have done the work.

20. *An Issue of Availability – What should be the extent of supervisor involvement and support at different stages of a doctoral research programme?*
   This very much depends on the needs of the student. Some students may require a lot of help at the beginning of the research programme to instil confidence, while they may find writing to be easy. In contrast, some students may require little help early on, but find great difficulty seeing their work as a substantial addition to the literature and need considerable assistance in achieving this. At the extremes, throughout the research programme some students require little help while others are always demanding.

21. *An Issue of Health – How long can a student be registered for a research degree?*
   There are time limits for all modes of study for research degrees. After the time limit has expired, then under normal circumstances a student would have to make a special case for registration to be extended. Such a case could be made on health grounds. If, however, this was due to a chronic medical condition, an extension might continue for a number of years. As long as the student provides medical certificates and can demonstrate some sort of progress in their project, then registration is likely to be extended. Whether a research project ever becomes out-of-date is another question.

22. *An Issue of Direction – At what point might a student be considered capable of working independently?*
   Independent work by a research student usually refers to the situation in which the student is able to proceed with the research project without needing to frequently consult the supervisor. In an ideal student–supervisor relationship, it is hoped that this situation would develop as the student continues to make progress, and in the latter stages of the project, this would be expected to be the norm. Of course, with each

student this may occur earlier or later depending on a number of factors.

23. *An Issue of Contract – Who bears the ultimate responsibility associated with the PhD write-up and submission?*

In general, as long as the student continues to make adequate progress in their research project leading up to the write-up and submission of the thesis, the decision to submit lies with the student. During this latter phase the supervisor continues to provide advice and guidance. Of course, the supervisor would be expected to read and comment on drafts of the thesis as it is being written. However, if the student so wishes, the thesis can be submitted without it being seen by the supervisor. Such an event would be very unusual and would not normally be in the student's best interests.

24. *An Issue of Priority – After a research student has completed their research, taken up employment but still has not written the thesis, whose responsibility is it to get it finished?*

It is probable that a supervisor will have only limited contact with a student who has left the university to take up full-time employment, even though that student will still be registered for a PhD with the university. The supervisor should try to maintain contact with the student as much as he possibly can and record all attempts. However, the ultimate responsibility for the write-up lies with the student. Of course, if all contact with the student has been lost for a considerable period of time and there was no evidence of any progress being made by the student, then the university would probably take steps to terminate the student's registration unless the student could make a case to prevent this.

25. *An Issue of Write-Up – At what point does a supervisor decide that there is sufficient research content for thesis completion?*

This is purely down to experience of the research field and an awareness of what the expectations are of the research degree. This is why it is important to take note of an experienced supervisor's recommendations. Moreover, it also explains why it would be particularly difficult for any research student to make this decision. Nevertheless, as discussed in question 23, the student makes the final decision as to the content and presentation of the thesis.

26. *An Issue of* Viva *Preparation – Should all research students be offered a mock* viva?

Once the thesis has been produced, the examiners need to know how much the research student understands the work. The only format for gaining that information is via the *viva* examination. Therefore, it is only fair and reasonable to expect that a student is fully prepared for the oral examination through a mock *viva*. Not only does this give the student the benefit of such an experience, it also allows the mock *viva* examiners to give constructive criticism while simulating an examination environment. Of course, if a student refuses the offer of such a mock *viva*, then that is their choice. However, under most circumstances this should be strongly recommended and taken seriously by both parties.

27. *An Issue of Identity – How much involvement should a student have in the choice of External Examiner?*
Ideally, the student should play some part in the selection of an External Examiner if only in the preliminary discussions about potential examiners, to ensure that they have not had inappropriate contact with someone who is being proposed as a possible External Examiner. The problem for a typical student is that they will not have the more intimate knowledge of a potential examiner's character which can influence the manner in which the *viva* is conducted. What should happen is that the supervisor selects the best examiner to give the student a fair but thorough examination. It is often very difficult for a student to know how best to achieve this without considerable supervisor input.

28. *An Issue of Alleged Fraud – What are the disadvantages of a student having only one supervisor?*
Absence of a supervisor can lead to problems for the student if there is no one else to go to for specific advice. Only one supervisor is also unhelpful if the student needs intensive guidance and the research develops across subject boundaries. Not surprisingly, one supervisor is often unable to give a balanced view on a topic which can be rather limiting for a student. The new Code of Practice (QAA 2004) recommendation that a student should have access to a supervisory team should be helpful in this situation.

29. *An Issue of Collaboration – Increasingly, students are being allocated more than one supervisor. How can a student be managed optimally by a supervisory team?*
There should always be a principal or main supervisor who has ultimate responsibility for the student even though there may be additional supervisors. The additional supervisors should provide specialist expertise and knowledge in different subject areas. However, the main direction for the research and responsibility for the write-up should lie with the principal supervisor. Therefore, overall, a supervisory panel should provide a broader knowledge base. At the same time, if this team is managed correctly and allows a good working relationship to develop with the student, more can be achieved than with a single supervisor.

30. *An Issue of Procedure – What is the role of the Internal Examiner in the* viva *and its aftermath?*
The role of the Internal Examiner depends on the institution's regulations. Nevertheless, normally their role is to ensure that the institution's *viva* examination procedures are upheld. They are also there to ensure fair and appropriate treatment by the External Examiner. Of course, they also have an examining role although this is usually less than that of the External Examiner. If minor corrections have to be made to the thesis, often the Internal Examiner checks that these have been completed before a recommendation to award the higher degree can be made.

Appendix 2: Use of Student–Supervisor Issues in a Workshop Setting

Although presented in this book as a series of Issues illustrative of problems that may arise in the graduate research student and supervisor relationship at the commencement, during the progress, and at the final writing-up stage, of a PhD programme, some of these Issues have been used by the authors in conjunction with the Staff Development Unit of the University of Sheffield, in day or half-day workshops delivered to staff members of various Faculties and departments within the university.

The Research Supervisor's Development Workshops at the University of Sheffield have aimed at:

1. developing and embracing effective and high-quality supervisory practices through the exploration of issues in research student supervision;
2. setting, maintaining and monitoring standards of provision and achievement for effective and successful research degree programmes;
3. increasing the knowledge and understanding of the supervisory and examining processes relevant to graduate research students.

The workshops are designed to review present practices, identify strategies for effective supervision of graduate research students, identify and resolve potential areas of conflict in the research student–supervisor relationship, clarify and effectively implement assessment requirements and provide a forum for the sharing of experiences and ideas between supervisors of graduate research students.

As used at the University of Sheffield, the Research Supervisor Development Workshops are appropriate across all Faculties, and are relevant for supervisors of full- or part-time graduate research students, home-based or overseas students, and local or remote-location students.

The general issues that can be covered in the workshops include:

1. The induction of graduate research students.
2. The management and monitoring of graduate research student progress.
3. The assessment of graduate research student progress.

4. Transfer from MPhil to PhD.
5. The supervisor–student relationship and its changing character with time throughout a PhD programme.
6. Thesis write-up.
7. Examiner selection, the *viva voce* examination and its aftermath, and appeals.
8. The changing nature of the higher degree (MPhil, PhD, New Route PhD, professional doctorate).

The programme of the workshops is designed to maximize skills development and the exchange of information and ideas between the participants and the workshop leaders. The workshops are practical and participative, capitalizing on the experience and expertise of both the workshop leaders and the participants. There are four loosely defined, wide-ranging topics that may be selected for any given workshop, but in practice, the Faculties or departments can request that the workshop covers topics that may be more relevant to their specific requirements, and these may be chosen from any of the general topics, subject to the constraints of time. The broad topics that may be addressed are:

1. First-year-student induction and progression up to, and including, transfer.
2. Years two and three – monitoring and assessing progress.
3. Years two and three – conflicts, disputes and contentious issues, their recognition and resolution.
4. The final stages – write-up of the thesis and the examination process.

Among a number of specific topics that are frequently requested to be covered in individual workshops, are supervisor availability; student–supervisor communication inadequacies; student motivation; student loss of confidence; direction; ownership and credit for the research work; problems at the writing stage; conduct and procedures of the examination process.

In practice, and dependent on Faculty or department request, the workshops are delivered as two-hour lunchtime sessions, or as half-day or full-day sessions. The Research Supervisor Development Workshops at the University of Sheffield, are normally attended by 15–20 participants, plus the two leaders and workshop organizers (the experienced supervisor and a senior member of the University's Staff Development Unit), directing and facilitating the progress of the workshop to maximize the exchange of information, ideas and outcomes. The most effective make-up of the workshop will consist of some participants who are experienced, and others who are relatively inexperienced, as supervisors of graduate research students within the particular discipline. The format adapted by the University of Sheffield for the conduct of the workshop in a two-hour lunchtime session, involves a short introductory period of about ten minutes, to allow for necessary introductions to take place, and for the facilitators to explain the workshop proceedings to the participants. The workshops are conducted in as informal a manner as possible and during the introduction, the participants are asked to arrange themselves into small groups of three to five.

In the second phase of the workshop, the groups of participants are provided with brief scenarios of the issues that will be explored. Usually, over a two-hour period, two issues can be covered and discussed in depth. The first issue, covered in the first hour, is provided to the participants as a situation scenario arising as a result of events that have taken place over a certain time period, usually consequent upon the interaction between a graduate research student and a supervisor. Each scenario concludes with a number of questions (usually three to five), pertaining to the events occurring in, and the development of the situation described in the scenario. Each scenario is presented from two viewpoints, one as perceived by the supervisor, and the other as perceived by the graduate research student. Half the participating groups receive the supervisor scenario, the other half the scenario as seen from the viewpoint of the student. The questions posed in the supervisor and student scenarios are different. At this stage, the groups will have seen only one viewpoint, either that of the student, or that of the supervisor. The groups of participants are now given time (about 15 minutes) to read the scenarios, discuss them within their groups (10 minutes) and to note points which may have arisen during their discussions that they may feel are relevant to the scenario and may have had a bearing on the situation that has culminated as a result of the events described.

At this stage the small groups will discuss issues arising from the scenarios, answer the questions posed, identify other issues or questions that may arise from their own experiences or concerns, and finally agree and summarize their findings as bullet points on display paper.

On completion of this phase of the workshop, the issues that have been raised and made into bullet points by each group are set up and displayed around the room so that they are visible to all participants in the workshop. The facilitators now take each point raised in turn, in a plenary session. Also, at this stage each group of participants are provided with, and read, the contraposed scenarios they have not yet seen (either that of the graduate research student or the supervisor). This phase of the workshop will involve informal discussion, guided by the facilitators, and accompanied by the sharing of any relevant experiences, comments or queries forthcoming from the floor, and will last approximately 20 minutes. At the conclusion the facilitators will summarize the main outcomes of the plenary session, at the same time allowing for questions or contributions from all the groups and participants, and also highlight any implications for good practice that have emerged during the discussions. The workshop participants can now reformulate into different groupings (still of three to five), a second situation scenario introduced, and the second hour of the workshop allowed to proceed along similar lines to the first.

At the conclusion of the workshop, simple evaluations forms are provided for completion by each of the participants and, at the University of Sheffield, the evaluation forms incorporate a question concerning any topics that arose during the session that the participant might wish to see followed up or expanded in future sessions.

To conclude this description of the Research Supervisor's Development Workshop, one of the case study scenarios is set out below in two sections, one from the viewpoint of the graduate research student, the other from that of the supervisor.

Aubrey's PhD – the student's first six months

My first meeting with my supervisor, Dr Rush, was really useful. He outlined the research project, awarded from Age Concern, which formed the basis of my acceptance as a graduate research student in the Department of Ageing Genetics at the University of Grimsville Medical School. He told me we would have a progress meeting each month and by six months I had to produce an up-to-date literature review for assessment. I would also be expected to give a talk on the progress of my research towards the end of the second semester. Having identified appropriate Research Training Programme (RTP) modules for me to attend, I was taken to the lab and introduced to Derek, a post-doc who would oversee my research on a day-to-day basis. I was informed I would be in good hands.

I really enjoyed myself over the next two months. I was busy with the lab work, and although most of this went well, one of the techniques central to my research refused to work. Derek advised me to keep at it as 'it will come out eventually'. I was also busy with my literature review and spent a lot of time collecting and reading anything that seemed relevant, and I had commenced one of the RTP units. I met monthly with my supervisor to discuss progress. He also dashed into the lab occasionally to ask how things were going. I assured him that all was well, despite a few technical problems. 'Teething troubles', he responded. I had a good Christmas vacation and did some skiing and winter walking in Scotland.

Early in January, an e-mail from Dr Rush postponed our meeting for the month. This really upset me, as Derek had indicated that he could probably have sorted out the techniques I hadn't yet got working. I was also worried about my literature review which at over 4,000 words seemed lacking in direction and clear focus. I consoled myself that at least part of my lab work was going well, and decided to do no more on my literature review until I had seen Dr Rush.

Towards the end of February when my supervisor appeared in the lab I asked to see him. 'I'm free for about 15 minutes,' he said, 'come to my office'. My mind was racing, but when we got there I wasted no time in telling him I was still having technical difficulties, I was concerned about my literature review and felt I'd made hardly any research progress. 'It's early days and these problems have a way of working themselves out,' he said, 'Stick at it!' He did offer to look at my literature review if I e-mailed it to him, before excusing himself for a departmental meeting due in five minutes and promised to see me again in March.

I watched him disappear down the corridor with mixed feelings. Hopefully I would get some feedback and guidance on my literature review but he had done nothing to allay my other concerns. I spent much of that evening and night trying to make my literature review look more respectable before the impending Easter holiday arrived when I could forget it all for a little while.

Q1. What do you think of the early establishment of Aubrey's research programme and its supervision?

Q2. What are your views on the type and amount of communication between the student and his supervisor to date?

Q3. Comment on the progress over the first semester.

Aubrey's PhD – the supervisor's first six months

I was pleased to have Aubrey as a PhD student. From what I'd seen of his undergraduate performance and his references, he appeared promising. At our initial meeting in the autumn semester he seemed on the ball as I outlined his research programme and informed him of the literature review deadline and the research report he would be expected to present in the summer. After discussing and selecting his RTP modules, and fixing up a date at the start of November for our next meeting, I introduced him to some of the research team in the lab.

I had my usual administrative commitments and a very busy teaching schedule coming up, plus, as meetings secretary of the Aged Social Health Society for this year, a conference to organize and bring into being next July. I knew this meant I would be unable to devote much 'hands-on' time to my research group over this period. However, I have a couple of good post-docs, and Anwar, one of my graduate students, now doing a PhD, is progressing well. As Aubrey's research work will be closely linked with Derek, one of my post-docs, as well as with Anwar's work, I felt I could safely leave the overseeing of his day-to-day work in their capable hands.

The next four months were bedlam for me. Christmas came and went virtually without my noticing it. I found myself loaded with extra teaching due to the illness of one of my colleagues; an epidemic of influenza in the city resulted in a lot of elderly individuals in difficulties and requiring my attention. To cap it all, my youngest child contracted mild meningitis early in the New Year. I was forced to postpone most of my research meetings over that time, including one with Aubrey in January, but he'd seemed OK when I occasionally came across him in the lab, and brief conversations with Derek confirmed this impression, although he was apparently encountering a few problems with some of the technology. I was pleased I had a research group that could support one another, and work along lines I had set out earlier, without requiring constant technical nannying and regular, wearing, moral support from me.

As things quietened down in February I ran into Aubrey when, as a result of a shortened meeting, I had a few minutes to spare, and decided to visit the lab on the spur of the moment. Although Aubrey indicated all was well, I thought in view of the meeting with him that I had postponed earlier, I should have a short discussion with him. I was quite surprised when, back in my office he appeared somewhat perturbed. After discussing matters with him, it seemed all was not going as well as he had led me to believe. A technique, important for his research, was not working for him, although it was being effectively used by both Derek and Anwar. Aubrey also claimed he had run into difficulties with his literature review, which I believed after our earlier meetings when we had discussed it briefly, should have been relatively straightforward for him. He apparently felt he had made little progress, but I knew he had completed a couple of experiments that looked promising even without using the full range of methodology.

By the time Aubrey had finished 'sounding off', it was time for my meeting. There was no way I could fully explore Aubrey's problems then and there, but I would have to briefly explore the situation with Derek to see if there was a real problem. I would also try to look through Aubrey's draft literature review and asked him to let me have this the following day. I reassured him he was progressing OK, and was still on track.

Q1. Has there been effective interaction between the supervisor and Aubrey during the supervisory process? Could more have been done?

Q2. What flaws can you see in the arrangements made for Aubrey's supervision over the first six months?

Q3. Do you think the supervisor's prioritization of workload is appropriate? If not, what should it be?

Q4. Comment on progress over the first semester. Should a supervisor have a role as a personal tutor?

Bibliography

British Educational Research Association (2004) *Revised Ethical Guidance for Educational Research*. Available at: http://www.bera.ac.uk/publications/guides.php

Delamont, S., Atkinson, P. and Parry, O. (2004) *Supervising the PhD: A Guide to Success*. Maidenhead: SRHE and Open University Press.

Dryden, C. and Jones, A. (1991) *Study of Postgraduate Supervision at the University of Sheffield*. University of Sheffield: Personal Skills Unit.

HEFCE (2004) *Circular Letter Number 18/2004, Postgraduate Research Degree Programmes*. London: HEFCE.

Higher Education Quality Council (1996) *HEQC Guidelines on the Quality Assurance of Research Degrees*. London: HEQC.

HM Treasury (2002) *SET for Success: The Supply of People with Science, Engineering and Mathematics Skills*. London: The Stationery Office.

Murray, R. (2002) *How to Write a Thesis*. Maidenhead: Open University Press.

Murray, R. (2003) *How to Survive Your Viva: Defending a Thesis in an Oral Examination*. Maidenhead: Open University Press.

NCIHE (1997) *Report of the National Committee of Inquiry into Higher Education* (the Dearing Report). London: Higher Education in the Learning Society.

Pearce, L. (2004) *How to Examine a Thesis*. Maidenhead: Open University Press.

Phillips, E.M. and Pugh, D.S. (2000) *How to Get a PhD: A Handbook for Students and Their Supervisors*, 3rd edn. Buckingham: Open University Press.

Quality Assurance Agency for Higher Education (1999) *Code of Practice for the Assurance of Academic Quality and Standards in Higher Education*. Gloucester: QAA for Higher Education.

QAA for Higher Education (2004) *Code of Practice for the Assurance of Academic Quality and Standards in Higher Education*. Section 1: Postgraduate Research Programmes. Gloucester: QAA for Higher Education.

Tinkler, P. and Jackson, C. (2004) *The Doctoral Examination Process: A Handbook for Students, Examiners and Supervisors*. Maidenhead: SRHE and Open University Press.

UK Council for Graduate Education ([1995] 2004) *Graduate Schools*, 2nd edn. London: UK Council for Graduate Education.

Index

Alleged Fraud (Issue of), 142–147, 178
Appeal (Issue of), 88–91, 175
Appeals, 50, 52, 90, 108, 164, 166
  see also complaints
Availability (Issue of), 101–105, 176

British Educational Research Association
  (BERA), 137

Collaboration (Issue of), 148–155, 178
Complaints, 108, 166
Conflict (Issue of), 12–16, 171
Contract (Issue of), 115–119, 177
Co-supervisor, 91, 109, 149, 151, 174
Culture (Issue of), 77–81, 174–175

Dearing Report, 4
Direction (Issue of), 110–114, 176–177
Distance (Issue of), 62–68, 174

English language, 21, 22, 24, 25, 26, 32,
  33, 34, 35, 36, 57, 58, 64, 66, 78, 79,
  126, 127, 162, 172, 173
English Language Training Centres
  (ELTCs), 36, 162
Equal Opportunities Policy, 141
External Examiner, 10, 39, 117, 127, 130,
  135, 139, 140, 143, 144, 147, 157, 158,
  159, 160, 161, 178

Funding (Issue of), 82–87, 175

Graduate Research Committee, 10, 165
Graduate Tutor, 10, 11, 16, 21, 25, 26, 31,
  42, 46, 47, 52, 61, 67, 72, 76, 80, 81, 89,
  90, 91, 92, 95, 100, 104, 105, 109, 114,
  123, 135, 145, 154, 155, 165, 171, 174

Head of Department, 9, 10, 14, 31, 43,
  44, 45, 46, 48, 51, 52, 57, 58, 59, 60, 61,
  67, 70, 71, 72, 73, 74, 75, 76, 79, 84, 85,
  92, 93, 95, 100, 103, 104, 114, 123, 143,
  145, 165

Health (Issue of), 106–109, 176
Higher Education Funding Council for
  England (HEFCE), 4

Identity (Issue of), 136–141, 178
Induction event, 20, 26, 29, 179, 180
Internal Examiner, 119, 127, 131, 135,
  139, 153, 155, 157, 158, 159, 160,
  178
Isolation (Issue of), 7–11, 171

Judgement (Issue of), 57–61, 173–174

Language (Issue of), 32–36, 172–173
Literature review, 7, 21, 22, 24, 28, 29, 33,
  36, 44, 49, 182, 183, 184

Management (Issue of), 73–76, 174
Meeting log, 52, 109, 171, 173
Mini-viva, 34, 163
Mock-viva, 126, 132, 133, 134, 135, 166,
  177
Monitoring of student progress, 7, 18,
  22, 28, 33, 48, 49, 50, 54, 73, 74, 80, 90,
  91, 93, 94, 95, 97, 99, 101, 102, 104,
  106, 109, 113, 118, 121, 123, 126, 134,
  137, 146, 148, 150, 154, 163, 164, 173,
  176, 179, 180, 182, 184

New Route PhD, 1, 5, 180
Non-compliance (Issue of), 17–20, 172

Office of the Independent Adjudicator
  for Higher Education, 4
Overseas students, 21, 25, 32, 33, 35, 36,
  43, 57, 62, 77, 80, 124, 127, 162, 172,
  174, 175
Ownership (Issue of), 97–100, 176

Part-time study, 27, 28, 29, 30, 31, 63, 66,
  67, 136, 163, 172
Personal tutor, 10, 45, 47, 174, 184
Personality mismatch, 15, 16, 74, 134

PhD with Integrated Studies, 1, 5
  see also New Route PhD
Plagiarism (Issue of), 21–26, 172
Priority (Issue of), 120–123, 177
Procedure (Issue of), 156–161, 178
Professional Doctorates, 1, 5, 62, 63, 65,
  66, 67, 180
Progress (Issue of), 53–56, 173

Quality Assurance Agency (QAA), 4, 165,
  171, 178

Research Assessment Exercise (RAE),
  70, 121
Research Councils, 1, 17
Research Training Programme (RTP),
  21, 22, 23, 25, 26, 42, 130, 133, 134,
  166, 182, 183
Role of the supervisor, 1

Scholarship conditions, 35, 173
Scrutiny (Issue of), 43–47, 173
Second supervisor, 11, 76, 91, 94, 109,
  126, 140, 165, 171
  see also co-supervisor
SET for Success report, 4
Stability (Issue of), 92–96, 175–176
Student expectations of supervisors, 2,
  162
Student independence, 17, 19, 55, 164,
  174, 175, 176
Student isolation, 3, 31, 42, 104, 172
Student motivation, 28, 53, 54, 56, 62, 65,
  66, 73, 75, 107, 122, 123, 164, 173, 180
Student selection, 25, 35, 41, 42, 46, 47,
  51, 76, 80, 90, 91, 146
Student-supervisor relationship, 2–3,
  20

Supervisor expectations of students, 3–4,
  20, 40, 81, 85, 104, 162
Supervisory teams, 3, 165

Teaching (Issue of), 69–72, 174
Thesis write-up, 41, 47, 65, 66, 68, 112,
  113, 115, 116, 117, 118, 119, 120, 121,
  122, 123, 129, 130, 139, 143, 144, 148,
  150, 151, 152, 153, 154, 155, 166, 177,
  180
Time (Issue of), 27–31, 172
Time management, 13, 16, 30, 31, 49, 63,
  64, 109, 114, 163, 175
TOEFL, 21, 32, 33, 34, 35, 36, 172, 173
Transfer (Issue of), 48–52, 173
Transfer from MPhil to PhD, 26, 28, 29,
  30, 34, 53, 73, 76, 83, 88, 92, 131, 135,
  138, 148, 163, 173, 180
Transfer Meeting, 19, 47, 48, 49, 50, 52,
  77
Transfer Panel, 8, 19, 34, 35, 39, 40, 41,
  42, 49, 50, 51, 52, 78, 80,
Transfer Report, 34, 35, 40, 42, 163

UK Council for Graduate Education, 5

Virtual Learning Environment (VLE),
  65, 66, 68
Viva preparation (Issue of), 129–135,
  177
Viva voce, 71, 119, 139, 140, 141, 142,
  143, 144, 145, 146, 147, 150, 151, 152,
  155, 156, 157, 158, 159, 160, 166, 178,
  180

Web CT, 65, 66
Write-Up (Issue of), 124–128, 177
Writing (Issue of), 37–42, 173

Related books from Open University Press

Purchase from www.openup.co.uk or order through your local bookseller

---

SUPERVISING THE DOCTORATE
A GUIDE TO SUCCESS
SECOND EDITION

Sara Delamont, Paul Atkinson and Odette Parry

- How can I get my students to produce good theses on time?
- My last student failed! What could I have done to prevent it?
- I am supposed to train the new supervisors in my faculty; where can I get some good ideas?

This new edition of *Supervising the Doctorate* still provides everything you ever wanted to know about the doctoral supervision but were afraid to ask! It includes:

- New material on supervising professional doctoral theses
- A new chapter on the changing policy context in higher education
- Latest research findings
- Experiential material from staff development sessions throughout the United Kingdom and New Zealand

Now that supervisor training is compulsory, this practical, no-nonsense handbook is essential reading for both the novice and the experienced higher degree supervisor. For novices there is a developmental sequence of advice, guiding them through all stages of supervision from the first meeting to the viva and beyond. For experienced supervisors there are fresh ideas on how to improve practice and solve problems.

Grounded in research, this book is invaluable to academics in all disciplines. At a time when there is increasing pressure to ensure 'quality' provision, to improve the doctoral completion rate, and to turn out employable graduates, the need for a practical guide is obvious. An essential item for every academic's bookshelf.

Contents
Preface and acknowledgements – A most persuasive piece of argument: introduction – Caught and held by a cobweb: getting the student started – The balance between tradition and progress: designing and planning a project – Old manuscripts: the literature review – Heavy and thankless task: overseeing the data collection – Disagreeableness and danger: keeping up student motivation – Contorted corkscrew: the getting and giving of judgement – An emotional excitement: writing up the thesis – A lack of genuine interest: choosing the right external and preparing the student for the examination – The brave pretence at confidence: launching students' careers – A rather unpromising consignment: selecting successful students and building a research culture – The very loftiest motives: institutional frameworks and audit cultures – Further reading – References – Index.

240pp   0 335 21263 8 (Paperback)   0 335 21264 6 (Hardback)

HOW TO EXAMINE A THESIS

Lynne Pearce

- What is involved in examining a research-based higher degree?
- What are the roles of the internal and external examiners?
- What are the hidden agendas of higher degree examining?
- What are the essential ingredients of a 'good' viva?

This handbook offers a revealing insight into the written – and unwritten – rules and regulations of higher degree examination in the United Kingdom today. Addressed directly to the examiners, it contains a step-by-step account of the different stages of the examination process in order to provide an insiders' guide into what to expect before, during and after the oral examination.

How to Examine a Thesis covers important issues such as:

- The power-relations between the two (or more) examiners
- Hidden agendas and foul play
- Examples of guidelines and regulations across different institutions
- Advice on MPhil as well as doctoral examinations

This book is essential reading for all higher degree examiners but is also of importance to those supervising, and studying for, higher degrees. Moreover, although the book focuses primarily on current practices in the United Kingdom, comparisons are drawn with continental Europe, Australia and the United States. Research degree examiners, supervisors and students throughout the world will find the book of considerable interest.

Contents

Acknowledgements – Introduction: The 'Rough Guide' to higher degree examining – Higher degree examining in the UK – Your appointment as examiner – Reading the thesis – Preparing for the viva – The viva – After the viva – Notes – Bibliography – Index.

136pp   0 335 21442 8 (Paperback)   0 335 21443 6 (Hardback)

THE DOCTORAL EXAMINATION PROCESS
A HANDBOOK FOR STUDENTS, EXAMINERS AND SUPERVISORS

Penny Tinkler and Carolyn Jackson

- What is the viva and how can students prepare for it?
- What should supervisors consider when selecting PhD examiners?
- How should examiners assess a doctoral thesis and conduct the viva?

The doctoral examination process has been shrouded in mystery and has been a frequent source of anxiety and concern for students, supervisors and examiners alike. But now help is at hand. This book sheds new light on the process, providing constructive ways of understanding the doctoral examination, preparing for it and undertaking it.

This book stands alone in the field due to the extensive research undertaken by the authors. During a four year project, interviews were conducted with candidates and academics from a wide range of disciplines through the United Kingdom. Outcomes and ideas from the research have been united to provide the most comprehensive information available.

Real life accounts and case studies are combined with useful advice, tasks and checklists to create an illuminating handbook. This user-friendly book is a vital resource for anyone involved in the doctoral process. No doctoral candidate, examiner or supervisor should be without it.

Contents
Acknowledgements – Introduction to the PhD examination process – Understanding the doctoral viva: what is it for? – Understanding the doctoral viva: how does it work? – Viva preparation: long term – Selecting examiners – Who attends the viva? roles and obligations – Examiners: should you examine? – Examiners: assessing a PhD thesis – Viva preparation: short term – Viva preparation: final stage – In the viva: candidates' perspectives – The viva: tips and issues for examiners – Post viva – References.

192pp   0 335 21305 7 (Paperback)   0 335 21306 5 (Hardback)

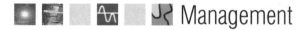